Topnotch Essays
On
AI And Law

Advanced Series On
Artificial Intelligence (AI)
And Law

Dr. Lance B. Eliot, MBA, PhD

DEDICATION

To my incredible daughter, Lauren, and my incredible son, Michael.

Forest fortuna adiuvat (from the Latin; good fortune favors the brave).

CONTENTS

Note: Visuals are collected together in Appendix B, rather than being interjected into the chapter contents, for ease of reading, enhanced flow, and to see the visuals altogether.

Dr. Lance B. Eliot

ACKNOWLEDGMENTS

I have been the beneficiary of advice and counsel by many friends, colleagues, family, investors, and many others. I want to thank everyone that has aided me throughout my career. I write from the heart and the head, having experienced first-hand what it means to have others around you that support you during the good times and the tough times.

To renowned scholar and colleague, Dr. Warren Bennis, I offer my deepest thanks and appreciation, especially for his calm and insightful wisdom and support.

To billionaire and university trustee, Mark Stevens and his generous efforts toward funding and supporting the Stevens Center for Innovation.

To Peter Drucker, William Wang, Aaron Levie, Peter Kim, Jon Kraft, Cindy Crawford, Jenny Ming, Steve Milligan, Chis Underwood, Frank Gehry, Buzz Aldrin, Steve Forbes, Bill Thompson, Dave Dillon, Alan Fuerstman, Larry Ellison, Jim Sinegal, John Sperling, Mark Stevenson, Anand Nallathambi, Thomas Barrack, Jr., and many other innovators and leaders that I have met and gained mightily from doing so.

Thanks to Ed Trainor, Kevin Anderson, James Hickey, Wendell Jones, Ken Harris, DuWayne Peterson, Mike Brown, Jim Thornton, Abhi Beniwal, Al Biland, John Nomura, Eliot Weinman, John Desmond, and many others for their unwavering support during my career.

Thanks goes to the Stanford University CodeX Center for Legal Informatics and the Stanford University Computer Science department for their generous support, and for the insightfual and inspirational discussions and feedback from my many fellow colleagues there.

And most of all thanks as always to Lauren and Michael, for their ongoing support and for having seen me writing and heard much of this material during the many months involved in writing it. To their patience and willingness to listen.

CHAPTER 1
INTRODUCTION TO
AI AND LAW

This book provides a series of compelling essays encompassing the burgeoning field of AI and the law. These essays are ostensibly standalone and do not require any prior familiarity with the AI and law topic. You are welcome to read the essays in whichever order you might prefer. The essays have been numbered and sequenced as chapters for ease of referring to the discussions and not due to any need to read one before another. The essays provide a helpful overview and entry point into the field of AI and law.

You will find the essays relatively easy to read and eschew arcane techno-terminology, aiming to layout the vital aspects in clear language and seeking to be readily grasped. The chosen topics entail the latest and hottest trends in the AI and law arena.

For those of you that are interested in knowing more about AI and the law in a deeper way, you might consider my other books:

- *"AI and Legal Reasoning Essentials"* by Dr. Lance Eliot
- *"Artificial Intelligence and LegalTech Essentials"* by Dr. Lance Eliot
- *"Decisive Essays on AI and Law"* by Dr. Lance Eliot
- *"Ingenious Essays on AI and Law"* by Dr. Lance Eliot
- *"Compelling Essays on AI and Law"* by Dr. Lance Eliot
- *"Incisive Research on AI and Law"* by Dr. Lance Eliot

The first two books are more akin to textbook-style orientations to the AI and the law field.

The other books are a further collection of my essays and the latter book contains my in-depth research papers (oriented toward legal and AI scholars). The books are available on Amazon and at major bookseller sites.

One of the most frequent questions that I get asked during my webinars, seminars, and university courses about AI and the law consists of what the phrase "AI and the law" actually refers to.

That's a fair question and deserves a useful answer. In a moment, I will borrow from my other books to provide an explanation about the meaning of "AI and the law" and then dovetail into a brief indication about each of the essays contained in this collection.

Per the essays, you'll end up seeing that there is a great deal of enthusiastic spirit for AI and the law, and likewise a sizable dollop of angst and trepidation about the intertwining of the two. In my view, whether you love it or hate it, there is no stopping the steamroller moving ahead that is going to infuse AI together with the law.

I would urge that any lawyer worth their salt ought to be learning about AI and the law. This will assuredly be especially important for those that are just now starting their legal careers, which I mention because the odds are that the convergence of AI and the law will have an especially pronounced effect throughout your lifelong legal efforts.

For those of you that might be going a more so academic route in the legal realm, rather than being a practitioner of the law per se, the beauty of AI and the law is that there is ample room for new research and a grand opportunity to make a demonstrative mark on the field. There are numerous open questions and plenty of challenges that provide abundant possibility for making a decided mark on this still nascent field of study.

Despite the fact that the field of AI and the law has been studied for many years, dating back to the beginning of the AI field itself, please be aware that we have only scratched the surface on this interweaving. Anyone with a desire to push the boundaries of these two realms will readily find plenty of rampways to do so.

If you are curious about the possible research avenues to pursue, make sure to take a look at my book on *AI and Legal Reasoning Essentials* since it provides a solid foundation on the research to-date and postulates what might be coming down the pike in future research activities, and then consider my book on *Incisive Research on AI and Law*. I bid you welcome to the field and wish you the best of luck in your endeavors.

I next provide a brief introduction to the field of AI and law, which echoes my thoughts as variously expressed in my other books and my various articles and postings.

AI And Law

In my viewpoint, Artificial Intelligence (AI) and the field of law are synergistic partners. The intertwining of AI and Law can generally be categorized into two major approaches:

- **AI as applied to Law**
- **Law as applied to AI**

Let us consider each of those two approaches.

AI As Applied To Law

AI as applied to law consists of trying to utilize AI technologies and AI techniques for the embodiment of law, potentially being able to perform legal tasks and undertake legal reasoning associated with the practice of law. Those scholars, experts, and practitioners that have this focus are using AI to aid or integrate artificial intelligence into how humans practice law, either augmenting lawyers and other legal professionals or possibly replacing them in the performance of various legal tasks.

Crafting such AI is especially hard to accomplish, problematic in many ways, and there have been and continue to emerge a myriad of attempts to achieve this difficult goal or aspiration.

The rise of LegalTech and LawTech, which is modern digital technology used to support and enable lawyers, law offices, and the like throughout the practice of law are gradually and inexorably being bolstered by the addition of AI capabilities.

There are many indications already of this trend rapidly expanding in the existing and growing LegalTech and LawTech marketplace. Notably, the potent AI and LegalTech/LawTech combination has been drawing the rapt attention of Venture Capitalists (VCs). According to figures by the National Venture Capital Association (NVCA), the last several years have witnessed VC's making key investments of over one billion dollars towards law-related tech startups, many of which have some form of an AI capability involved.

Most of the AI developed so far for LegalTech and LawTech is only able to assist lawyers and legal professions in rather modest and simplistic ways. For example, AI might speed-up the search for documents during e-discovery or might enhance the preparation of a contract by identifying pertinent contractual language from a corpus of prior contracts.

Where the field of applying AI to law is seeking to head involves having AI that can perform legal-minded tasks that human lawyers and other legal professionals perform. In essence, creating AI systems that can undertake legal reasoning. This is commonly referred to as AI for Legal Reasoning (AILR).

In a sense, legal reasoning goes to the core of performing legal tasks and is considered the ultimate pinnacle as it were for the efforts to try and apply AI to law. It is undoubtedly one of the most exciting areas of the AI-applied-to-law arena and one that holds both tremendous promise and perhaps some angst and possible somber qualms.

Law As Applied To AI

The other major approach that combines AI and law focuses on the law as applied AI. This is an equally crucial perspective on the AI and law topic.

Sometimes this is also referred to as the **Governance of AI**, though there are those that believe that to be a somewhat narrower perspective on the topic. In any case, the focus is primarily on the governance of AI and how our laws might need to be revised, updated, or revamped in light of AI systems.

You likely already know that AI is experiencing quite a resurgence and has become a key focus of the tech field, along with gaining attention throughout society. AI is being rapidly infused into a wide variety of industries and domain specialties, including AI in the financial sector, AI in the medical domain, and so on.

This rapid pace of AI adoption has opened the eyes of society about the benefits of AI but also has gradually brought to the forefront many of the costs or negative aspects that AI can bring forth. Some assert that our existing laws are insufficient to cope with the advances that AI is producing. Thus, the need to closely examine our existing laws and possibly revamp them for an era and future of ubiquitous AI.

Expected Impacts

Let's consider how AI and the law can impact those in the AI field, and also contemplate how it can impact those in the field of law.

If you are an AI specialist, you should certainly be interested in the AI and law topic, either due to the possibilities of advancing AI by discovering how to leverage AI into the legal domain or due to the potential of how existing and future laws are going to impact the exploration and fielding of AI systems.

If you are a lawyer or legal specialist, you ought to be interested in the AI and law topic too, for the same reasons as the AI specialist, though perhaps with some added stake in the game.

What is the added stake?

If AI can ultimately become advanced enough to practice law, there is concern by some that it could potentially replace the need for human lawyers and other human legal-related law practitioners.

Some liken this to the famous and telling remark about commitment as exhibited via a chicken and a pig. A chicken and a pig are walking along and discussing what they might do together, and the chicken offers that perhaps they ought to open a restaurant that serves ham-n-eggs. Upon a moment of reflection, the pig speaks up and says that if they did so, the chicken would only be involved (making the eggs), while the pig would end-up being fully committed (being the bacon).

In that sense, AI specialists in this topic are involved, while legal specialists and lawyers are committed. Meanwhile, for those of you squarely in the field of law, lest you think that AI specialists are to be spared the same fate of being overtaken by AI, you will be perhaps surprised to know that there are efforts underway to craft AI that makes AI, such as in the field of Machine Learning (ML), a specialty known as AutoML, which could potentially put human developers of AI out of a job. What is good for the goose is good for the gander. Or, it might be that what is bad for the goose is equally bad for the gander.

About These Essays

Now that you've gotten an initial synopsis regarding the topic of AI and law, let's take a moment to briefly take a look at the essays assembled for this decisive collection.

Chapter 1 – Introduction To AI And Law

Key briefing points about this chapter:

- This book is a collection of crucial essays about AI and the law

- The essays are provided as numbered chapters (the sequence is not essential)

- AI and the law consist of two key facets

- One facet is AI as applied to the law (a mainstay of this collection)

- The other facet is applying the law to AI (i.e., governance of AI)

Chapter 2 - AI & Law: Explainable AI (XAI)

Key briefing points about this chapter:

- Explanations are an integral part of our daily lives
- We are expected to provide explanations, and we expect to receive explanations
- Proffering explanations is a lot harder than it seems
- AI systems are increasingly being tasked to provide explanations, known as XAI
- There are several crucial dimensions of the law pertaining to the XAI matter

Chapter 3 - AI & Law: Reversing False Memories

Key briefing points about this chapter:

- Legal forensics concentrates extensively on the nature of human memories
- Lawyers know that a court case can rise or fall based on the veracity of witness memories
- A recent research study examined the implanting of memories, along with their reversal
- Though a limited study, the results provide interesting insights for attorneys
- AI applied to the law ought to leverage such studies about human cognition and memory

Chapter 4 - AI & Law: Antitrust and AI

Key briefing points about this chapter:

- The bailiwick known as antitrust is rather vaguely defined and wide-open to interpretation

- This means that at times antitrust behavior might freely exist and fail to be spotted

- There is also the chance of falsely labeling antitrust when it is not altogether deserved

- Using AI and Machine Learning, a recent study explored the underpinnings of antitrust

- The described research is handy as an important step toward AI in the antitrust realm

Chapter 5 - AI & Law: Legal Aid Services

Key briefing points about this chapter:

- Some assert that the tagline of no money, no lawyer, no justice is altogether true

- Laudable ongoing efforts attempt to provide low-cost or even entirely free legal services

- However, there is still a presumed unbalanced supply-demand for legal services

- AI is increasingly being infused into LegalTech and might be a potential answer here

- The future might consist of low-cost or freely provided AI-based legal advisory systems

Chapter 6 - AI & Law: Bring Your Own Algorithm

Key briefing points about this chapter:

- A famous saying is to never bring a knife to a gunfight
- Unpacking this sage advice reveals insights about how to arm yourself in a duel
- Lawyers are in duels when it comes to their court cases
- Everyday uses of Bring Your Own Algorithm (BYOA) are starting to arise
- Get ready for legal-oriented BYOA, coined as Bring Your Own Legal Algorithm (BYOLA)

Chapter 7 - AI & Law: Percolation of the Law

Key briefing points about this chapter:

- Percolation comes up in our daily activities such as brewing a cup of coffee
- Most of the time, we think of percolation as a physical or chemical process
- There is also information percolation, for which the field of law is a grand exemplar
- Today's legal percolation can be construed as being good and being bad
- With the advent of AI in the law, legal percolation could change dramatically

Chapter 8 - AI & Law: Rule of Law

Key briefing points about this chapter:

- Discussions about the rule of law are aplenty in our news feeds these days

- It is handy to consider what is meant by referring to the rule of law

- A recent report examines the rule of law and highlights a new twist involving AI

- We need to make sure that AI abides by the rule of law

- And likewise, ensure that AI in the law will not subvert the rule of law

Chapter 9 – AI & Law: British Nationality Act

Key briefing points about this chapter:

- A foundational research paper in the 1980s explored the British Nationality Act

- The researchers sought to transform the law into AI-based programming code

- At the time, the Prolog programming language was considered a top means for doing so

- This seminal work has been oft-cited and provided a foundation in AI and the law

- The researchers recently received the inaugural Stanford CodeX Prize 2021

Chapter 10 - AI & Law: Legal API

Key briefing points about this chapter:

- Application Programming Interfaces (APIs) have been in the news recently

- SCOTUS handed down a ruling in the decade-long case of Google vs. Oracle

- Rather than focusing on the decision, let's consider API's all told

- APIs are essential to the future of LegalTech

- And APIs will also be crucial to the advancement of AI and the law

Chapter 11 - AI & Law: Ramifications of Bad AI

Key briefing points about this chapter:

- There is much discussion these days about *AI for Good*

- This has startled people into realizing that there is also the potential of *AI for Bad*

- Regulators are considering passing new laws to stem the possibility of Bad AI

- The EU supposedly is considering a severe penalty for firms that promulgate Bad AI

- Attorneys versed in AI and the law are going to find themselves facing a goldmine of work

Chapter 12 - AI & Law: Computable Contracts

Key briefing points about this chapter:

- Contracts are typically a key element of any legal practice and the work efforts therein

- Computing aids the drafting of legal contracts, albeit somewhat simply so

- Law practices are adopting Contract Lifecycle Management (CLM) tools

- Computable contracts are being advanced via legal scholars and LegalTech vendors

- AI is ultimately an integral component in the future of such contracts

Chapter 13 – AI & Law: C-Suite Buy-in

Key briefing points about this chapter:

- Most companies require C-suite buy-in or approval for the by-function budget requests

- As a longtime CIO/CTO, I've worked hand-in-hand with Chief Legal Officers (CLOs)

- Trying to get the C-suite to spend toward LegalTech has been an ongoing uphill battle

- A recent EY Law and Harvard Law School survey showcases those difficulties

- Leveraging and in a sense exploiting AI-based LegalTech can inure a budgetary buy-in

Chapter 14 – AI & Law: Standards for LegalTech

Key briefing points about this chapter:

- Worldwide shipping is a marvel partially due to the advent of shipping container standards

- By establishing standards for sizes of shipping containers the global shipping effort eased

- In the legal field, there are nascent standards such as the well-known LEDES for billing

- Other new standards are being formed such as for NDAs, contracts, and the like

- It is time to forge forward on standards for the AI aspects of the legal field and LegalTech

Chapter 15 - AI & Law: No Code

Key briefing points about this chapter:

- Lawyers and the legal profession are nowadays discussing code aplenty

- There is the notion of law-as-code

- There is the case made by some that lawyers ought to be coders

- A differing view asserts that lawyers should be using no-code toolsets

- The bottom-line about no-code is to do your homework and keep your eyes open

Chapter 16 – AI & Law: Human Signs of Dishonesty

Key briefing points about this chapter:

- Robot judges continue to be a topic of keen discussion and at times heated debate

- A disturbing and misleading trend aims to say that robot judges can detect dishonesty

- Predictions are that robot judges will use sensors to assess body language and human signs

- This seems somehow glorious but is outstretched and misguided

- Time to set the record straight and make sure that robot judges are aiming correctly

Chapter 17 - AI & Law: Soft Law on AI

Key briefing points about this chapter:

- Soft law is oftentimes a precursor to officially formalized hard laws

- The arising of soft law tends to occur when shoring up new domains or innovations

- A slew of soft law has emerged in the burgeoning field of AI

- Arizona State University (ASU) College of Law has established a database of soft law about AI

- This database is a veritable treasure trove, publicly available, and can be sliced-and-diced

Chapter 18 - AI & Law: Regulating AI

Key briefing points about this chapter:

- AI systems keep being developed and fielded by the thousands upon thousands

- Some liken this to the days of the wild west, whereby existing laws are deficient

- As a result, many AI systems seem lawless or sneakily skirt the law

- Proposals exist about shoring up existing laws to make sure that AI gets reined in

- Consider a set of legal principles regarding AI that The Alan Turing Institute proposes

Chapter 19 - AI & Law: Primer on AI and Law

Key briefing points about this chapter:

- There is some confusion about what "AI and the law" constitutes

- Some see only a part of the whole and become focused solely on a particular piece

- Thus it is useful to take a holistic look at the entirety of AI and the law

- This quick primer depicts a two-way street framework

- In short, there is: (1) AI applied to the law, and (2) Law applied to AI

More About This Book

For anyone opting to use this book in a class or course that pertains to these topics, note that Appendix A contains suggestions about how to use the book in a classroom setting.

Furthermore, Appendix B contains a set of slides that depict many of the salient points made throughout the book.

In some of my prior books, I've interspersed the slides into the chapter contents, but feedback by readers has generally been that readers prefer to not have the textual flow become disrupted by the slides, and instead prefer to have the supplemental material assembled altogether into an appendix.

To make sure that you are aware of those added materials, you'll notice that the ending of each chapter provides a quick reminder about the visual depictions that are available in Appendix B.

And so, with this overall orientation to the nature and structure of this book in mind, please proceed to read the essays and learn about the field of AI and law. I'm truly hoping that you'll find the essays mentally engaging and stimulative to the nature of how the law is being practiced and what the future of the law might become.

Note: *For supplemental materials depicting the aspects discussed in this chapter, refer to Appendix B, which contains various augmented diagrams, charts, and additional related facets of relevance.*

CHAPTER 2

AI & LAW: EXPLAINABILE AI (XAI)

Key briefing points about this essay:

- Explanations are an integral part of our daily lives

- We are expected to provide explanations, and we expect to receive explanations

- Proffering explanations is a lot harder than it seems

- AI systems are increasingly being tasked to provide explanations, known as XAI

- There are several crucial dimensions of the law pertaining to the XAI matter

Introduction

Time to dive into the pool and see what is going on with the nature of explanations, including explaining explanations and ensuring that explanations are truly being explanatory. That might seem like a somewhat flippant imperative remark, but there is a serious uproar emerging about the importance of explanations.

Notably, the legal field is smackdab in the center of it all.

Let's back up for a moment and start the tale at its proper beginning.

In daily life, we take for granted that explanations are all around us. You take your car to a local repair shop and the automotive mechanic might explain why your car has gone kaput. Later that day, you visit with your physician and get an explanation for why your shoulder has been hurting lately. Upon getting home for the evening, your child explains why they did poorly on their latest math test at school.

Explanations galore!

In the legal field, explanations are abundantly infused into just about everything encompassing the practice of law. Your client explains why they did what they did. Score a point for hearing an explanation. You have to craft a legal case that proffers explanations of your legal position on the matters at hand. Another point scored, this time for writing an explanation. A judge hands down a court decision and includes an explanation articulating the legal reasoning used. That's a scored point on your part for reading a likely in-depth and legally complex explanation.

The everyday use of explanations is generally taken for granted. Sometimes an explanation is freely provided by someone, while in other instances you have to tease an explanation out of a person. For example, a physician might just tell you to go home and rest, failing though to explain why the prescriptive act of resting is material to your hurting shoulder. As such, you might have to inquire of the doctor as to what is the explanation for that particular piece of advice.

Overall, we can easily open up Pandora's box on this topic by taking a moment to contemplate the myriad of nuances associated with explanations. Suppose the physician goes into tremendous detail covering the technical facets of human anatomy when explaining the issues associated with your shoulder. If you don't have any prior medical training, the explanation is bound to go over your head. On the other hand, imagine that the doctor simply says "trust me" and won't provide any semblance of an explanation. That's another sour indication about explanations and the manner in which explanations are oftentimes badly framed and inadequately conveyed.

XAI And The Law

The legal profession has its own difficulties associated with explanations.

Laypeople that don't know about the law and arcane legal matters are apt to be confused by deeply crafted explanations that embody all kinds of legal jargon. That can be problematic.

When standing in the courtroom and being asked to provide an explanation to a judge, an attorney has to tune their explanation to the circumstances of the case and as seemingly best honed to the style and preferences of the judge. This can make or break your case.

The overarching point is that pinning down the particulars of what is an explanation, how to best compose an explanation, the right ways to express an explanation, and so on, ostensibly is an exceedingly slippery and amorphous phenomenon.

The reason this is recently coming to the forefront is due to the advent of AI.

Suppose that you visited your physician, and it was an AI system rather than a human being. Would you expect the AI to be able to explain why it has recommended that you get some rest, having made such a recommendation after assessing your shoulder? Seems like you would decidedly want an explanation.

Explainable AI has its own catchy acronym now too, namely labeled as XAI. Some assert that all AI will inexorably have to utilize XAI and be programmed to explain itself, in all circumstances and in varied modes that fit the situation and the needs of the human desirous of receiving an explanation.

This brings us to the legal side of things.

There is the potential for legal requirements requiring that AI provide explanations, such as via consumer protection laws.

Liability can potentially arise too for those providing AI systems that fail to provide explanations. That is one dimension of the legal XAI consideration.

Another dimension is found within the field of law itself. AI that is crafted specifically for legal reasoning purposes is likely to be expected to provide suitable explanatory expositions. The use of AI capabilities including Machine Learning (ML) and Deep Learning will profoundly impact the law and become a vital tool for attorneys, judges, and the entire judicial process. For details on this and other AI and law topics, see my book entitled "AI and Legal Reasoning Essentials" (available on Amazon).

As emphasized in a research paper about XAI and the law, researchers Katie Atkinson, Trevor Bench-Capon, and Danushka Bollegala assert that legal cases imbue a right-to-explanation: "In a legal dispute there will be two parties and one will win and one will lose. If justice is to be served, the losers have a right to an explanation of why their case was unsuccessful. Given such an explanation, the losers may be satisfied and accept the decision or may consider if there are grounds to appeal. Justice must not only be done, but must be seen to be done, and, without an explanation, the required transparency is missing. Therefore, an explanation is essential for any legal application that is to be used in a practical setting" (as expounded in their paper entitled "Explanation in AI and Law: Past, Present, and Future" published in the journal *Artificial Intelligence*).

In the early days of combining AI and the law, there were AI-augmented LegalTech systems that used rules-based or expert systems technologies, which provided an intrinsic means to automatically generate an explanation. Likewise, pioneering proof-of-concept systems in the field of AI and law such as TAXMAN, HYPO, CATO, made use of case-based reasoning and conveniently enabled the generation of explanations.

Today's Machine Learning systems are less amenable to producing explanations.

This is partially due to the utilization of inherently complicated computational pattern matching models and the arcane mathematics involved. Should those ML systems be let off the hook about needing to provide explanations?

Researchers Bernhard Waltl, Technical University of Munich, and Roland Vogl, Executive Director for the Stanford Center for Legal Informatics make a demonstrative case that omitting XAI or trying to somehow after-the-fact cobble a supplemental XAI to an Algorithmic Decision Making (ADM) system is not going to cut the mustard, namely that XAI must be intrinsically included: "In our framework, explainability is not treated as an optional characteristic or additional external property that can be "plugged-in" to machine learning classifiers like adding a new component or application to a set of given functions and capabilities. Instead, it is an intrinsic property of every ADM that can be improved and enhanced just as other (performance) attributes can be improved" (as identified in their research paper entitled "Explainable Artificial Intelligence: The New Frontier in Legal Informatics").

Conclusion

I could go on and on, nearly all day long, discussing and debating the topic regarding explanations and AI, but then again, just as you might seek a shorter abridged explanation when your shoulder is having some mild aches and pains, perhaps we'll end the *explanation about explanations* at this juncture.

Just know that there is a lot more on explaining to do on explanations and you can readily dive into explanations to your heart's deepest content.

Note: *For supplemental materials depicting the aspects discussed in this chapter, refer to Appendix B, which contains various augmented diagrams, charts, and additional related facets of relevance*

CHAPTER 3
AI & LAW:
REVERSING FALSE
MEMORIES

Key briefing points about this essay:

- Legal forensics concentrates extensively on the nature of human memories

- Lawyers know that a court case can rise or fall based on the veracity of witness memories

- A recent research study examined the implanting of memories, along with their reversal

- Though a limited study, the results provide interesting insights for attorneys

- AI applied to the law ought to leverage such studies about human cognition and memory

Introduction

They say that memories light the corners of your mind and last an eternity. That is undoubtedly a quite touching and heartwarming sentiment.

Unfortunately, it might not hold water.

A recent research study entitled "Rich False Memories Of Autobiographical Events Can Be Reversed" provides some fascinating tidbits about the implanting or concoction of memories and then took a second round to see if those false memories could be undone or reversed (the paper appears in the *Proceedings of the National Academy of Sciences*, posted March 30, 2021, authored by Aileen Oeberst, Merle Wachendorfer, Roland Imhoff, and Hartmut Blank).

From a legal perspective, the nature of human memories is an extremely vital matter and can potentially make or break a case. There are often crucial circumstances whereby an attorney is betting on the veracity of a witness and assumes (hopes) that upon questioning in the courtroom that the person will be able to hold true to their claimed memories. Of course, on the other side of that fence, there are circumstances in which a lawyer is aiming to reveal those memories of a witness as ostensibly false and should not be relied upon.

Memories, love them or hate them, depending on how they seem to aid your case or undermine your case. The good news is that human memories can be seemingly vibrant and unforgettable, allowing someone to be wholly confident that their recall is completely accurate and valid. The bad news, or perhaps additional good news, entails the aspect that memories can be fragile and tend to decay over time.

The reason that the brittleness of memories can be good news is that it provides an opening to undercut the claims made by someone that does not align with your side of a case. Did the person perhaps make up aspects of the memory, doing so to fill in gaps or embellish the memory to seem more palatable or favorable in their own mind? Someone can do so via inadvertently shaping or reshaping their memories, plus they can outrightly falsify a matter by purposely inventing memories that never actually existed.

That is a bit of a conundrum.

A false memory could be intentionally created by someone and they know it to be false.

Then again, a false memory might have been somewhat subliminally created and the person is not purposely trying to pull a fast one per se. If you have someone that swears on their personal oath that something happened as based on their memory of the event or activity, you can't readily discern whether they are knowingly lying or might believe wholeheartedly in a self-adjusted or self-devised memory that they think is of an original origin.

Going Deep Into Memories

Let's rachet up this memory dilemma by considering the notion of implanting memories.

The implanted memory could in a sense be false or it could be true. For example, I find out from your parents that you got paint all over your face and hands when as a toddler you opted to touch a newly painted fence near your home. When I ask you about this, and now in your capacity as a grown adult, you profess that you don't remember the incident.

Upon mulling it over, you begin to say that perhaps you do remember the humorous circumstance. Indeed, now that you are concentrating on the event, you are absolutely sure that you have memories of the occasion. Yes, definitely, you are quite sure that it happened.

This could be considered a true memory, since it was an actual event that happened to you and the memory was nudged to the forefront by the reminder that it occurred. A critic might try to argue that the memory is somewhat false in that you didn't recall it immediately and therefore this raises perhaps some qualms about the veracity of the memory. Nonetheless, it was a real incident, and you are now claiming that you do recall it.

Get ready for the shocker in this tale.

Suppose I then tell you that your parents did not indicate that you had gotten paint on you as a child.

In fact, upon being asked whether any such incident ever happened, they insist that no such thing ever happened. Thus, I have fed you a false line and you seemed to take it hook-line-and-sinker. You have created your own false memory.

Score one for implanting memories.

You might be steamed at this kind of trickery. Some people might even continue to cling to the "implanted" memory and become insistent that it did happen. Nobody likes to be fooled.

Others might fold their cards and sheepishly admit that they weren't quite sure about the memory, but that with the presumed assurance by their parents, they faintly were able to reconstruct what they thought was a true event. They are now willing to reverse or undo the implanted memory.

Score a point for reversibility.

The research study on false memories stated this: "Human memory is fallible and malleable. In forensic settings, in particular, this poses a challenge because people may falsely remember events with legal implications that never actually happened." Various techniques were used to induce false memories of the participants in the experiment, and then reversal techniques were used, leading to this conclusion: "One strong practical implication is that false memories can be substantially reduced by easy-to-implement techniques without causing collateral damage to true memories."

Being able to probe into the nuances of human memory is vital for those that practice law. In addition, the future of the law will entail the advent of Artificial Intelligence (AI). AI has to do with being able to craft computer-based systems that can perform in ways that humans can. This entails deeply exploring the nature of human cognition and human memory capabilities. For details on this and other AI and law topics, see my book entitled "AI and Legal Reasoning Essentials" (available on Amazon).

Conclusion

There is the famous sage saying that the best thing about memories is making them.

Perhaps a caveat to that wisdom is that the best thing about memories is that they can be originated, <u>and</u> they can decay, they can be implanted, they can be reversed, and altogether be flexible and malleable. That makes memories quite versatile, though indubitably presents grand challenges to those that practice the law.

.

———

Note: *For supplemental materials depicting the aspects discussed in this chapter, refer to Appendix B, which contains various augmented diagrams, charts, and additional related facets of relevance.*

Dr. Lance B. Eliot

CHAPTER 4

AI & LAW:

ANTITRUST AND AI

Key briefing points about this essay:

- The bailiwick known as antitrust is rather vaguely defined and wide-open to interpretation

- This means that at times antitrust behavior might freely exist and fail to be spotted

- There is also the chance of falsely labeling antitrust when it is not altogether deserved

- Using AI and Machine Learning, a recent study explored the underpinnings of antitrust

- The described research is handy as an important step toward AI in the antitrust realm

Introduction

Assemble a bunch of attorneys into a room and ask them what antitrust means. This will likely produce a wide-ranging consensus around a vague notion of what antitrust constitutes but will not get you into any all-hands fully agreeable ironclad specifics.

Let's explore those difficulties and how they create some serious problems.

Probably the most common notion of antitrust is that any firm exercising undue and relatively unabridged marketplace power could be construed as skating on thin ice when it comes to possibly violating antitrust laws. By slapping the label of being monopolistic onto overbearing anti-competitive behavior, entities falling into the realm of presumed antitrust activities are subject to regulatory action and at times loudly denounced by the media and society all told.

All is fair in love and war, but when it comes to businesses and the marketplace, the assertion is that antitrust laws are the valiant protector to ensure that bona fide competitive forces are enabled and purposely engineered to economically provide a balanced playing field. Some say that antitrust enforcement makes for healthy competition. We are all seemingly outsized beneficiaries of an antitrust watchful eye.

Others though argue that antitrust can be overly predatory and potentially inhibit or strangle competition, causing firms to be sheepish and timid out of concern for getting slammed as being antitrust. There is a kind of stickiness associated with getting branded as a potential antitrust wrongdoer. Once a firm is tainted by the antitrust brush, they often find themselves under the antitrust scrutiny microscope and forced to explicitly and extraordinarily justify each and every move they make.

It is even conceivable that an antitrust-tainted snowball effect will arise, whereby an antitrust accusation begets an antitrust investigation, which inexorably begets an antitrust prosecution. Some suggest that this sequence is altogether inevitable, regardless of whether there is any merit to the initial antitrust claim or vocalized complaint. Like a crazed out-of-control machine that cannot stop after the start button has been pressed, the antitrust bandwagon blindly runs forward and steamrolls over both those that are truly antitrust and the innocents that aren't antitrust but that get caught up in the trust-busting fever.

The thing is, not everyone necessarily agrees as to the specific and particular aspects of being antitrust. Vast volumes of legal writings about antitrust can ostensibly convince you of all sorts of conditions and preconditions that potentially merit the antitrust badge. Beauty is in the eye of the beholder, and so too is the nature of antitrust. One person's viewpoint of antitrust might or might not comport with those of another. Antitrust can be a quite slippery armament to get your arms around.

Maybe some AI can help with this.

Antitrust Machine Learning To The Rescue

In a fascinating research study entitled "Gleaning Insight from Antitrust Cases Using Machine Learning," researchers Giovanna Massarotto, Adjunct Professor at the University of Iowa, and Ashwin Ittoo, Associate Professor at the University of Liege, proffer a close-up look at the nature of antitrust (published under the auspices of the *Stanford Computational Antitrust Project* as directed by Dr. Thibault Schrepel).

The research considered whether there might be pertinent characteristics that can be extracted from existent antitrust cases and then utilized to identify essential underlying patterns evocative of what constitutes antitrust behavior. This is an intriguing question and one that might be aided via the use of state-of-the-art AI capabilities. They describe their work in this manner: "Our study aims to tackle this question by building and testing an antitrust machine learning (AML) application based on an unsupervised approach, devoid of any human intervention. It shows how a relatively simple algorithm can, in an autonomous manner, discover underlying patterns from past antitrust cases by computing the similarity between these cases based on their measurable characteristics."

This is yet another notable example of how AI is increasingly being applied to all areas of the law.

Furthermore, the use of AI capabilities including Machine Learning (ML) and Deep Learning will profoundly impact the practice of law and become a vital tool for attorneys, judges, and the entire judicial process. For details on this and other AI and law topics, see my book entitled "AI and Legal Reasoning Essentials" (available on Amazon).

When undertaking the use of Machine Learning, the data chosen for scrutiny has to be carefully selected and thoughtfully prescreened. For the research by Massarotto and Ittoo, they examined a wide array of antitrust case data, and ultimately ended up with seventy-two antitrust proceedings that were sourced directly from the FTC official website and spanned a nearly fifteen-year period of 2005 to 2019.

Here is how they classified the cases on an antitrust determination basis: "We identified the following categories of anticompetitive conduct: exclusionary conduct (A); predatory conduct (B); refusal to deal (C); tying conduct (D); price fixing (E); rebates (F); discriminatory practice (G); customer allocation agreement (H); pay for delay (I); disruption in the bidding process (J); agreement orchestration (K); invitation to collude (L); agreement not to compete (M); unlawful exchange of information (N); concerted practices (O); conspiracy (P); no poach (Q); and no anti-competition (NOCOND)."

They also categorized the FTC-ordered antitrust remedies.

All of this was used to create a robust dataset that would enable the Machine Learning algorithm to try and computationally cluster cases. As stated by the researchers: "The algorithms project the data, here antitrust cases, as vectors in a multi-dimensional space. Then, the distance between cases is estimated based on the variables characterizing each case. Finally, similar (less distant) cases are grouped into clusters while minimizing a criterion, such as the error."

After extensive runs of the AI system, the ML revealed several key clusters.

One important caveat about today's Machine Learning is that it is mathematically oriented and not necessarily able to overtly "explain" or provide a human-understandable interpretation that showcases a logical basis for the calculated results. The researchers closely examined the clusters and came to a reasoned conclusion about the work performed: "Our study shows that a relatively basic ML approach can automatically discover the most important underlying characteristics of antitrust cases and identify similarities between those cases."

Conclusion

This provides a handy step toward using AI as part of the antitrust realm. By using Machine Learning in this manner, legal scholars have a new tool to explore the antitrust universe. Regulators and agencies such as the FTC can also leverage AI and ML in their efforts.

Hopefully, the added use of AI will aid in going after the bad actors that are rife with antitrust shenanigans. This might likewise reduce the chances of chasing after good actors that are ostensibly being unfairly dinged for being unfair when they are actually being fair. The fish caught up in the everyday antitrust fishing net can perhaps be more discerningly separated into the rotten menaces versus the innocuous catch-and-release variety.

.

Note: *For supplemental materials depicting the aspects discussed in this chapter, refer to Appendix B, which contains various augmented diagrams, charts, and additional related facets of relevance.*

CHAPTER 5
AI & LAW:
LEGAL AID
SERVICES

Key briefing points about this essay:

- Some assert that the tagline of no money, no lawyer, no justice is altogether true

- Laudable ongoing efforts attempt to provide low-cost or even entirely free legal services

- However, there is still a presumed unbalanced supply-demand for legal services

- AI is increasingly being infused into LegalTech and might be a potential answer here

- The future might consist of low-cost or freely provided AI-based legal advisory systems

Introduction

No money, no lawyer, no justice.

That's an oft-cited qualm about the justice system being unequal toward those that have money and can afford justice versus those that lack money and ostensibly cannot get sufficient justice. This concern has been exemplified in the noble catchphrase of *pro bono publico*, inuring a call of public service upon all those that practice the law.

As succinctly stated in 2014 by U.S. Supreme Court Associate Justice Ruth Bader Ginsburg: "Lawyers have a license to practice law, a monopoly on certain services. But for that privilege and status, lawyers have an obligation to provide legal services to those without the wherewithal to pay, to respond to needs outside themselves, to help repair tears in their communities."

Providing free or ostensibly nearly-free extremely low-cost legal services is a difficult challenge to pull off and one that continues to be daily discussed and wrangled with.

There are laudable efforts such as the Free Access to Law Movement (FALM). FALM is a collective of "legal information systems projects across many countries to provide free online access to legal information such as case law, legislation, treaties, law reform reports, and legal scholarship" (see the FALM website for further info). Spurred into the formulation in 1992 by the Legal Information Institute (LII) at the Cornell Law School, via the auspices of Thomas Bruce and Peter Martin, this longstanding desire to make legal information freely available is certainly admirable and altogether praiseworthy.

The U.S government has established a webpage devoted to ways that free and low-cost legal aid can be obtained (see www.usa.gov/legal-aid). This potentially provides a means to spread the word about available resources for those seeking legal services at notably affordable prices, albeit perhaps on an entirely free basis in some instances too.

Consider for a moment that legal services can be composed of two major components, namely the availability and applicability of legal information, and the availability and utilization of legal advice.

A properly licensed legal advisor provides legal advice, along with indubitably having to rely upon and obtain useful and usable legal information. Meanwhile, legal information unto itself is only a partial solution since there is seemingly inevitably a need to apply legal advice to whatever legal information might be existent.

The Crucial Equation

The point is that legal services could be construed as consisting of this straightforward equation: *Legal Services = Legal Advice + Legal Information*.

The purveyor of legal advice is almost necessarily going to need legal information. Even if the legal advice is being proffered for free, there is still a chance of costs associated with the legal information portion of the equation. In a similar vein, the odds are that if one somehow did perchance have free legal information, they are nonetheless likely stinted due to the potential cost for obtaining commensurate legal advice to turn that legal information into legal action.

When you think of the word "information" the next thought ought to immediately be the notion of information technology. Information technology has made access to information a boon in comparison to years in the past that kept information housed physically in geographically distant places and generally made getting access quite unaffordable. The pervasive technology of today enables information to be readily at hand, via smartphones, laptops, and an array of computing capabilities.

The imagery of referring to "legal advice" is bound to bring forth a picture in your mind of lawyers diligently toiling away at dispensing their legal acumen. This is an exceedingly labor-based task today. Some would assert that the laborious facets of serving as an attorney are what makes getting legal advice expensive or at least not at an extremely low-cost or on a free basis. Though many valiantly do provide their legal advice for free or at a low cost, it would seem that the potential supply of such legal aid is woefully below the amount of potential need for such services (an out-of-whack supply-demand conundrum).

Just as tech can come to play for the legal information side of the equation, we can nowadays also look toward tech on the legal advice portion too.

As eloquently stated by Jason Solomon, Executive Director, Stanford Center on the Legal Profession: "For example, we need new TurboTax-like tools for legal services" (see his article entitled "Getting More Legal Help to Californians" posted on Law.com). This would presumably provide both a legal advisory capacity and legal information, coupled together into a readily available app. Per Solomon: "Such tools are starting to emerge, but they are too hard to build given current restrictions around who can own them and who can answer questions from consumers."

In California, there are State Bar working groups underway regarding the rules around providing such legal services: "These are important efforts, but they need to be accelerated. The risks of moving slowly are high – people improperly denied unemployment benefits, minority-owned businesses unable to access PPP loans, unlawful evictions" stated Solomon.

My research efforts are focused on applying Artificial Intelligence (AI) to the law and seeking to make the legal advice portion of the equation increasingly automatable. The use of AI capabilities including Machine Learning (ML) and Deep Learning will profoundly impact the law and become a vital tool for attorneys, judges, and the entire judicial process. For details on this and other AI and law topics, see my book entitled "AI and Legal Reasoning Essentials" (available on Amazon).

Recent efforts to apply AI to the legal information aspects have been encouraging, including the DataLex platform: "We consider the constraints that the requirement of 'free' imposes (on both the legal assistance sector and on LIIs), including on what types of free legal advice systems are sustainable, and what roles LIIs may realistically play in the development of such a commons of free legal advice" (as depicted in "Utilizing AI In The Legal Assistance Sector" by Andrew Mowbray, Philip Chung, and Graham Greenleaf in *Computer Law & Security Review*).

Conclusion

AI-based legal reasoning has the potential for reducing the amount of human labor involved in undertaking the provisioning of legal advice. Attorneys could be augmented by AI systems and thus the computing performs the bulk of the legal service and the lawyers act as validators or supervisors. Eventually, it is assumed that AI-based legal reasoning systems will autonomously dole out legal advice.

Admittedly, there is no guarantee that this would assure that legal services are going to be free or low-cost, but it would seem to boost the odds for such nearly free legal aid services to be freely available and perhaps free all told.

———————

Note: *For supplemental materials depicting the aspects discussed in this chapter, refer to Appendix B, which contains various augmented diagrams, charts, and additional related facets of relevance.*

CHAPTER 6
AI & LAW:
BRING YOUR OWN ALGORITHM

Key briefing points about this essay:

- A famous saying is to never bring a knife to a gunfight

- Unpacking this sage advice reveals insights about how to arm yourself in a duel

- Lawyers are in duels when it comes to their court cases

- Everyday uses of Bring Your Own Algorithm (BYOA) are starting to arise

- Get ready for legal-oriented BYOA, coined as Bring Your Own Legal Algorithm (BYOLA)

Introduction

Two lawyers are going head-to-head in the courtroom. This is reminiscent of the Old West and the kinds of gunslinger duels that we've seen time and again in movies and TV shows.

Speaking of such battles, here's a sage piece of advice that you'd undoubtedly come across: Never bring a knife to a gunfight.

That's a rather famous or possibly infamous line that you've undoubtedly heard countless times. Numerous variants exist such as saying don't bring a knife to a gunfight or make sure to bring a gun to a gunfight rather than a knife.

The idea behind this bit of everyday memorable wisdom would seem to be that you should go into a skirmish armed on an equal basis as your opponent. If your opponent has a gun, you ought to also be carrying a gun. The presumed problem with possessing a knife in such a circumstance is that you are going to get gunned down and be unable to adequately engage in the battle via having nothing more than a measly knife.

This certainly seems altogether sensible.

Attorneys are apt to relish looking under-the-hood at all kinds of commonplace debate-oriented postures or arguments that people tend to concoct. You've likely not had an occasion to unearth the actual sensibility underlying the knife-and-the-gun catchphrase.

Let's unpack it together.

The popular cable show *Mythbusters* decided to examine the matter and proffered an eye-opening result. The two primary provocateurs in the show opted to carry out a simple experiment. One of them was armed with a knife. The other was armed with a holstered gun. They did a faceoff in which they were theoretically going to try and harm each other.

After an indication to start the experiment, the one armed with the knife ran straight at the other that was trying to unholster their gun and expeditiously shoot at the madly rushing figure. Turns out that if the running person with the knife was within about sixteen to eighteen feet of the gunslinger, the knife holder would reach the gun-toting person before getting shot. In that case, presumably, the knife-wielding person would win by overtly stabbing the person brandishing the gun and ergo end the contest.

In brief, a knife can win during a gunfight, depending upon the circumstances (as they say, your mileage may vary).

For those of you that are movie buffs, you might also remember the notable scene in the original version of *The Magnificent Seven* that introduces the character, Britt, as played by actor James Coburn. Britt is essentially forced into dueling with a gunslinger, during which Britt chooses to use only a knife. As a spoiler alert in case you've not seen the movie, be forewarned that I am about to tell you what happened. In a tense face-to-face confrontation, a signal is emitted to start the contest and Britt immediately throws his readied knife at the gunslinger. The thrown knife in this case is faster than the actions of the gun shooter, and the knife fatality strikes the gunslinger without Britt getting shot at all.

Okay, we've pretty much taken apart this claimed contention to never bring a knife to a gunfight and have hammered it to the floor.

If you only have a knife, you still might prevail. Generally, the truism would seem to be that you should seek to match fire-with-fire, as it were, and therefore bring a gun, though the garnering of a knife still provides chances at succeeding if used in particular ways. Something that might seem to be undervalued can be used in shall we say creative ways to boost the potency involved.

One supposes that the best piece of wisdom might be to bring both a gun and a knife, thus perhaps being able to choose whichever will work effectively and decisively in the matters at play. Arm yourself with a multitude of potentially viable armaments to be well-prepared for whatever might arise.

Unleashing The BYOLA

This brings us to the emergence of BYOA, a trend known as Bring Your Own Algorithms.

With today's smartphones, you can arm yourself with algorithms or apps that can be your knowledge-wielding veritable knife-or-gun in dealing with the daily chores of life.

Suppose you go to see your physician and the doctor tells you to take a certain kind of medication for your sore shoulder. Via a medical-oriented BYOA on your smartphone, you bring up an app that warns about side effects and you then ask the doctor some probing questions accordingly. On your own, you wouldn't have known to ask about the side effects. You didn't have the needed knowledge or armament to actively participate in the "contest" at hand.

BYOA can solve that problem.

Here's the kicker.

We are going to increasingly have BYOA for the legal field.

Yes, akin to a miniaturized computerized lawyer in a bottle, there are going to be apps that people will arm themselves with for contending with the law. Whenever getting jammed-up in a legal situation, out will come a handy BYOA. In the case of the legal profession, I've been referring to this as the Bring Your Own Legal Algorithm or BYOLA. A notable phenomenon that will gradually appear as an offshoot of traditional BYOA.

The BYOLA is going to get better and better as a result of infusing AI.

The use of AI capabilities including Machine Learning (ML) and Deep Learning will profoundly impact the law and become a vital tool for attorneys, judges, and the entire judicial process. For details on this and other AI and law topics, see my book entitled "AI and Legal Reasoning Essentials" (available on Amazon).

Non-lawyers will be using the BYOLA.

And you can bet your bottom dollar that lawyers will find themselves also making of such apps or algorithms. In a sense, it would be as though you are carrying around a legal colleague that is ready to aid you in complex legal matters, doing so 24x7 and whenever and wherever you might be. Judges would equally find the BYOLA useful.

This open's a legal Pandora's box, that's for sure. Are these BYOLA providing legal advice and if so, does that constitute the unauthorized practice of the law? How will they be regulated? How will they be validated?

Conclusion

Well, here's the final rub.

If during a court case, the opposing legal counsel is using a BYOLA, and you are not, will you be the proverbial unarmed fighter in a heated gunfight? Even if you do have a BYOLA, suppose theirs is better than yours is, in which case, you are maybe carrying a knife to a gunfight. Better make sure you know what you have armed yourself with, aiming for legal practice preservation and becoming the well-armed and ostensibly winning legal party.

Note: *For supplemental materials depicting the aspects discussed in this chapter, refer to Appendix B, which contains various augmented diagrams, charts, and additional related facets of relevance.*

CHAPTER 7

AI & LAW:

PERCOLATION OF THE LAW

Key briefing points about this essay:

- Percolation comes up in our daily activities such as brewing a cup of coffee

- Most of the time, we think of percolation as a physical or chemical process

- There is also information percolation, for which the field of law is a grand exemplar

- Today's legal percolation can be construed as being good and being bad

- With the advent of AI in the law, legal percolation could change dramatically

Introduction

You get up in the morning and wander into your kitchen. While still half-asleep, you put in the coffee filter of your coffee maker. In a sense, percolation has just become an important part of your day.

47

How so?

Well, you undoubtedly use percolation when making coffee. Yes, the coffee filter serves as a strainer or a form of percolation that produces a tasty cup of java. The early morning serving of your wake-up beverage boosts your slumbering wits and gets you ready to tackle those legal cases anxiously stacked on your desk.

The Latin roots of percolation indicate that this handy word suggests the notion of filtering or straining something. Most of the time, we tend to associate percolation with a physical or chemical process. For example, rainwater percolates through the soil and can become purified or filtrated as a result of the percolation process.

There is another way to think about percolation, namely as a filtering process associated with information. In some sense, this is of course a physical activity, though it also has a kind of less tangible aura since it is information-based rather than say a more obvious physical aspect such as rainwater or coffee.

If you read a morning news blog to find out what's happening in the world, the odds are that the posted content will have been percolated or filtered in some fashion. Perhaps a story about the latest employment statistics has gone through a multitude of editing hands, having been shaped and reshaped by the time it appears at the top of your blog updates.

That's an example of information percolation.

Upon reflection, you might realize that the legal field has a lot to do with information percolation. Let's consider that the lower courts are ostensibly information percolators, and they act as a form of filtration for that which might ultimately reach the top courts. Legal cases that eventually land at the U.S. Supreme Court have usually been extensively percolated, undergoing a rather lengthy and arduous journey via the legal gauntlet or filtering across our court system.

It is easy to assume that this legal percolation is undisputedly good and altogether favorable in that it seemingly makes sure that only "purified" matters reach the highest court in the land. Keep in mind that percolation does not necessarily imply goodness. Though filtering for coffee and also for rainwater is generally a desirable activity, there can readily be conditions under which percolation is troubling and the outcome is undesirable.

Percolation is a neutral kind of process per se and as such can be turned toward either good or bad, at times speeding up or slowing down whatever is being filtered, plus the result could be that the bad stuff has been filtered out and only good stuff remains, or there is the undeniable potential that the good stuff gets inadvertently drained out and the bad stuff remains.

In-Depth Legal Percolation

The topic of legal percolation takes center stage in a fascinating research paper entitled "Percolation's Value" in the February 2021 issue of the *Stanford Law Review,* authored by legal scholars Michael Coenen, Professor of Law, Seton Hall University Law School, and Seth Davis, Professor of Law, University of California, Berkeley School of Law. As they decisively point out: "Few legal metaphors enjoy more prominence than that of a legal issue 'percolating' through the lower courts until the Supreme Court is ready to resolve it."

Their paper thoughtfully analyzes the ongoing debate about the role of information percolation in the law field. A typical gut assumption by many is that percolation is handy and altogether helpful to all legal matters.

But, as the researchers stridently emphasize: "The process has its costs, to be sure: Issue percolation can yield delay, repetitive litigation, nonuniformity, and prolonged uncertainty about the content of the law. But proponents of the process maintain that those costs are often outweighed by the benefits that percolation provides. Percolation, the argument goes, has value. And the federal courts would do well to take its value into account."

Notable jurists have landed on both sides of the matter. Associate Justice William Rehnquist noted in the mid-1980s that percolation "makes very little sense in the legal world in which we live." Justice Clarence Thomas decried national injunctions as "preventing legal questions from percolating through the federal courts." And so on.

Per the conclusions of this insightful research study: "Our overall take is a qualifiedly skeptical one. Without discounting the possibility that some instances of percolation might confer benefits that exceed their costs, we are not convinced that, as a general matter, the Supreme Court should go out of its way to ensure that multiple lower courts offer answers to legal questions that the Court already intends to decide." And their bottom line is this: "At best, we think, percolation's benefits will outweigh its costs under limited and contingent conditions—conditions not likely to replicate themselves across a broad range of cases."

Shifting gears, the future of the law will entail the advent of AI-based legal reasoning systems. The use of AI capabilities including Machine Learning (ML) and Deep Learning will profoundly impact the law and become a vital tool for attorneys, judges, and the entire judicial process. For details on this and other AI and law topics, see my book entitled "AI and Legal Reasoning Essentials" (available on Amazon).

Discussions about percolation in the legal field tend to focus on existing processes and how the court system incorporates percolation as we conceive of it currently. Of course, that attention to today's world is quite practical and sensible, since it is a conception of legal percolation that we can presently see and touch, along with taking into account for our existent court cases.

Some have argued that the emergence of AI in the field of law will radically impact the practice of law and the nature of adjudication. For example, there are assertions that via AI the possibility of generating all legal variants to a case and its arguments will be heightened. Rather than having a case wind its ways slowly through the courts, a push of the button could presumably illuminate the entirety of the underlying legal arguments.

What might AI then do to the legal percolation process?

One obvious claim is that legal percolation will occur on an exceedingly rapid basis. No longer will cases take months, years, or even decades to bounce around within the courts. Nearly overnight, a case could be routed to the Supreme Court, along with an accompanying and exhaustive indication of all identifiable arguments associated with the case.

Conclusion

On the surface, this would appear to be alluring. As they say, justice delayed is justice denied. Not everyone is quite so enthusiastic about this alteration to legal percolation. Speed alone does not necessarily lead to a desirable outcome. Some believe we will, later on, reminisce about the good old days, when legal percolation took its sweet time.

Time will tell.

––––––––––

Note: *For supplemental materials depicting the aspects discussed in this chapter, refer to Appendix B, which contains various augmented diagrams, charts, and additional related facets of relevance.*

CHAPTER 8
AI & LAW:
RULE OF LAW

Key briefing points about this essay:

- Discussions about the rule of law are aplenty in our news feeds these days

- It is handy to consider what is meant by referring to the rule of law

- A recent report examines the rule of law and highlights a new twist involving AI

- We need to make sure that AI abides by the rule of law

- And likewise, ensure that AI in the law will not subvert the rule of law

Introduction

It sure seems like everybody is discussing the rule of law.

We all talk about it and the news is constantly bringing up whether someone is perchance *above* the law rather than presumably being subject to the law. It seems as though we are nowadays always on the edges of our seat about the rule of law.

What does it actually mean to refer to the rule of law?

A description given by the Administrative Office of the U.S. Courts indicates that the "rule of law is a principle under which all persons, institutions, and entities are accountable to the laws that are: Publicly promulgated, equally enforced, independently adjudicated, and consistent with international human rights principles."

Much of the time, our focus is on people and the rule of law. Did that person abide by the rule of law or did they go beyond the rule of law? Of course, we also can have angst when companies or other kinds of entities seem to veer from the rule of law. The expectation is that the rule of law will be all-encompassing and there ought not to be anyone or anything that sits outside the rule of law.

What about AI?

Yes, my question is whether Artificial Intelligence (AI) is to be considered within the scope of the rule of law. Should AI systems be considered subject to the rule of law? That is the big question currently being bandied about.

I would guess that your first thought would be that it is obvious and readily assumed that AI must be subject to the rule of law. There would not seem to be any basis for arguing otherwise. Since the rule of law was said to include all persons, institutions, and entities, this seems to be a large enough umbrella to encompass AI too.

Be aware that there is no kind of AI today that approaches human sentience in terms of human-like intelligence capabilities. Some look to the future and assert that such AI will eventually exist, but even if so, presumably the notion of "persons, institutions, and entities" would still sufficiently contain AI too.

As a quick aside, when thinking about AI and the law, there are two major perspectives to contemplate. One perspective involves how AI will be applied to the law, such as LegalTech systems that will make use of Natural Language Processing (NLP), Machine Learning (ML), and other AI technologies. The use of AI capabilities will profoundly impact the law and become a vital tool for attorneys, judges, and the entire judicial process.

For details on this and other AI and law topics, see my book entitled "AI and Legal Reasoning Essentials" (available on Amazon).

The other key perspective entails how the law applies to AI.

In essence, our existing laws might not be suitable to cover the nuances associated with AI systems. Some believe that we need to modify our laws to ensure that AI is clearly bounded by the rule of law. The concern is that existing laws seem to allow for loopholes that provide a kind of escape hatch for AI. Potentially, the courts might decide that AI is not in the scope of our existent rule of law.

This takes us back to the qualm about nobody being above the law. Well, perhaps we should phrase it as nobody and nothing can be above the law. All things, including the vaunted AI, will need to be definitively scoped within the rule of law, else AI systems might be devised that go against the grain of what we expect for societal behavior as grounded by the rule of law.

Rule of Law And AI

A recent report entitled "Artificial Intelligence, Human Rights, Democracy, and the Rule of Law" provides some interesting insights into the matter of AI and the rule of law. Co-authors of the report were David Leslie, Christopher Burr, Mhairi Aitken, Josh Cowls, Mike Katell, and Morgan Briggs, and was prepared by The Alan Turing Institute on behalf of the Council of Europe.

Here is what the report says about AI and the rule of law: "AI systems must not undermine judicial independence, due process, or impartiality. To ensure this, the transparency, integrity, and fairness of the data, and data processing methods must be secured."

If you carefully interpret the indication, note that there is an emphasis on AI as a bad actor that could somehow potentially undermine the rule of law. You could say that this covers both the AI-as-applied to the law and likewise the law-as-applied to AI side of the coin.

Envision that AI is used in the courts and embraced by judges, attorneys, and the like. It could be that the AI systems end up undercutting our judicial activities and perhaps imbue biases that trample on the rule of law. Members of the legal profession might not overtly realize that the AI is acting in this foul manner. Please realize I am not ascribing anthropomorphic properties to AI, and merely pointing out that arcane algorithms that are based on complex mathematics and computational elements might be inscrutable per se and therefore have hidden biases that are not readily detectable.

The report provides several proposed key obligations for countries that might adopt the principles of AI and the rule of law.

For example: "Member States must ensure that AI systems used in the field of justice and law enforcement are in line with the essential requirements of the right to a fair trial. To this end, they should ensure the quality and security of judicial decisions and data, as well as the transparency, impartiality, and fairness of data processing methods. Safeguards for the accessibility and explainability of data processing methods, including the possibility of external audits, should be introduced to this end."

You might be under the assumption that those developing AI systems would certainly realize the importance of ensuring that the AI abides by the rule of law. Regrettably, that is a false assumption and there are many pell-mell and rushed efforts toward putting AI into use that is not being properly vetted and validated.

Conclusion

In addition, some purposeful wrongdoers will assuredly opt to use AI as a type of legal-busting Trojan horse, incorporating hidden properties that are intentional violations of the rule of law. Those perpetrators taking such a route might have their fingers crossed that no one will be the wiser about their surreptitious inoculation of AI systems.

In brief, if we want AI to be subject to the rule of law, it is time to make sure that the emergence of AI is kept within that rubric. We decidedly do not want to find ourselves having let the horse out of the barn before putting in place needed and appropriate precautions.

————————

Note: *For supplemental materials depicting the aspects discussed in this chapter, refer to Appendix B, which contains various augmented diagrams, charts, and additional related facets of relevance.*

CHAPTER 9

AI & LAW:

BRITISH NATIONALITY ACT

Key briefing points about this essay:

- A foundational research paper in the 1980s explored the British Nationality Act

- The researchers sought to transform the law into AI-based programming code

- At the time, the Prolog programming language was considered a top means for doing so

- This seminal work has been oft-cited and provided a foundation in AI and the law

- The researchers recently received the inaugural Stanford CodeX Prize 2021

Introduction

Let's take a look at the past and for which we might also divine a glimpse into the future.

The British Nationality Act was passed in 1981 and shortly thereafter was used as a means of showcasing the efficacy of using Artificial Intelligence (AI) techniques and technologies, doing so to explore how the at-the-time newly enacted statutory law might be encoded into a computerized logic-based formalization. A now oft-cited research paper entitled "The British Nationality Act as a Logic Program" was published in 1986 in the prestigious *Communication of the ACM* and subsequently became a hallmark for subsequent work in AI and the law.

Those that are immersed in present-day efforts of intertwining AI and the law owe a debt or proper homage to this pioneering work from the 1980s.

I bring up this foundational work because co-authors Robert Kowalski, Fariba Sadri, and Marek Sogot were honored at this year's *CodeX FutureLaw 2021* annual conference for their pioneering efforts (the event took place online on April 8, 2021, and video recorded sessions are available for viewing). The esteemed researchers were augustly named as the inaugural winners of the Stanford CodeX Prize. *FutureLaw* is undertaken each year in the Spring by the Stanford Law School and the Stanford CodeX Center for Legal Informatics and focuses on the present day, predicted future, and prior cornerstone efforts underpinning the realm of computational law and LegalTech.

Let's take a quick look at some key facets of the landmark research paper.

Firstly, there were several other efforts already underway in that era that were trying to apply AI to the law but oftentimes used predominantly made-up examples rather than tackling actual legislature-derived and officially approved statutory laws. Though using concocted exemplars was certainly helpful, there was a sense of urgency about seeking to use real-world legalese and moving into the realm of messiness and complexity thereof.

As the paper stated about choosing the British Nationality Act: "The act embodies all the characteristics of statutes in general: syntactic complexity, vagueness, and reference to previously enacted legislation. In the course of this article, we will describe how the text of a large part of the British Nationality Act 1981 was translated into a simple form of logic, and we will examine some possible applications of this translation."

The work that they undertook was handy as a large-scale attempt at translating laws into computer-based logic that could then be run or executed. In other words, this is more than simply putting text into a computer system. The notion is that the logic of the law can be encompassed by the coding and therefore the law can be utilized as though it is active and able to be interpreted and applied.

This can ostensibly be used after the fact once a law already exists. The researchers pointed out that such formalized computer-based logic enactment can also be used when laws are initially devised or being drafted: "It means that an executable, logic-based representation of rules and regulations can be used not only to apply the rules but to aid the process of drafting and redrafting the rules in the first place."

Their research effort was aimed at the core mechanics of transforming legal rules into a form of computer-based logic. This provides a layer for subsequently building more advanced capabilities incorporating AI-based legal reasoning: "Finally, we should stress once again that we have not addressed the broad and much more difficult problem of simulating legal reasoning. Rather, we have concentrated on the limited objective of implementing rules and regulations to apply them mechanically to individual cases."

The Use of Prolog

The vaunted research paper provided snippets of the programming code developed and which implemented in a programming language known as Prolog.

Consider an example as based on this legalese portion of the Act: "A newborn infant who, after commencement, is found abandoned in the United Kingdom shall, unless the contrary is shown, be deemed for the purposes of subsection (1): (a) to have been born in the United Kingdom after commencement and (b) to have been born to a parent who at the time of the birth was a British citizen or settled in the United Kingdom."

This is the Prolog code that they devised to represent this indication:
> x is a British citizen
> if x was found as a newborn infant abandoned in the U.K.
> and x was found on date y
> and y is after or on commencement and not [x was not born in the U.K. after or on commencement]
> and not [x was not born to a parent who qualifies under 1.1 at time of birth]

For details on this and other AI and law topics, including a rudimentary explanation about Prolog, see my book entitled "AI and Legal Reasoning Essentials" (available on Amazon).

Conclusion

Per the famous sage wisdom by George Santayana, we must make sure to acknowledge and remember the past: "Progress, far from consisting in change, depends on retentiveness. Those who cannot remember the past are condemned to repeat it."

Our deepest thanks ought to go to the many legal scholars, legal professionals, and AI developers that have labored to make progress in the realm of AI and the law, and it is important to provide a tip of the hat from time to time to ensure that we remember and build upon those revered prior efforts accordingly.

Note: *For supplemental materials depicting the aspects discussed in this chapter, refer to Appendix B, which contains various augmented diagrams, charts, and additional related facets of relevance.*

CHAPTER 10
AI & LAW:
LEGAL API

Key briefing points about this essay:

- Application Programming Interfaces (APIs) have been in the news recently

- SCOTUS handed down a ruling in the decade-long case of Google vs. Oracle

- Rather than focusing on the decision, let's consider API's all told

- APIs are essential to the future of LegalTech

- And APIs will also be crucial to the advancement of AI and the law

Introduction

API's have gotten their moment in the sun, as it were.

Hard to believe that the topic of Application Programming Interfaces (APIs) managed to get worldwide attention, but it did. This rather nerdy topic garnered some bold and brash headlines recently when the U.S. Supreme Court ruled on the infamous case of *Google LLC v. Oracle America, Inc.* (No. 18-965, decided on April 5, 2021), which pertained to the use of the arcane and ostensibly vaunted Application Programming Interface matter.

Dating back nearly a decade, this frolicking case has been bandied back-and-forth and generally hidden from view for anyone other than pure techies. Those within the tech world have fervently watched the case with intense interest, on the edge of our seats, and anxiously endured the roller coast ups and downs that have taken place during this ten-year-long elongated and bumpy path. Meanwhile, most of the rest of the world has not given much ado over the apparently obscure considerations involved.

That being said, there was unquestionably a lot at stake since the technology underpinning much of today's apps and advanced computer systems are reliant upon APIs. Believe it or not, you could construe those APIs as the potential Achilles heel or as the Herculean hero of modern-day computing.

What is an API, you might be wondering?

The SCOTUS ruling defined API's this way: "An API allows programmers to call upon prewritten computing tasks for use in their own programs." This might seem somewhat vague and perhaps leaves you feeling hollow and wholly unsure of why there is such a hullabaloo over the API mechanism.

A further depiction in the SCOTUS ruling caused me to cringe and I'm sure the same happened to anyone truly versed in programming and software development, but nonetheless, this is how APIs were characterized: "Imagine that you can, via certain keystrokes, instruct a robot to move to a particular file cabinet, to open a certain drawer, and to pick out a specific recipe. With the proper recipe in hand, the robot then moves to the kitchen and gives it to a cook to prepare the dish. This example mirrors the API's task-related organizational system."

The passage adds that "importantly, you do not need to know the recipe's contents, just as a programmer using an API does not need to learn the implementing code."

All About APIs

Anyway, moving beyond carping about this outstretched description, the notion is that when a programmer wants to make use of someone else's program, a convenient means to do so consists of invoking an available API. This means that the program being used would need to have beforehand established what their "interface" or application accessible portal consists of (this notification can be done via posting instructions that indicate the nature of the interface that is being made available for use).

I might be writing a program that needs to sort numbers from low to high in magnitude, and instead of writing the code myself, I find someone that has made such a program available for use. This saves me the effort of having to write a sorting program. Furthermore, even if I wrote a sorting program, it might not be as optimized and cleverly devised as a program that was written by top-notch experts specializing in sophisticated sorting algorithms.

The program that provides the sorting capability would be established so that you could merely provide that available program with a list of values and it would provide back to you those values in sorted order. The sorting could be done in either a low-to-high or a high-to-low sequence. As such, when the sorting program is utilized, you need to give it an indication of which way you want the sorting to occur, along with providing the list of values to be sorted.

The programmers publish what their API is, and you make use of that API to run their app accordingly from your own program.

Note that there isn't a requirement that programmers provide APIs for their software, though it is generally a wise thing to proffer. If you want others to leverage your software, it makes sense to set up a bunch of APIs.

What can eventually happen is that an entire plethora of other software will all become reliant upon your programs, and you can potentially make a ton of money by either charging them for this usage or that your software will become widely popular and thus you can monetize via other means.

By and large, providing a set of APIs will enable the emergence of a thriving third-party add-on ecosystem and potentially turn your software into a kind of superstar.

I'm not going to delve into the SCOTUS ruling and merely mention that in a sense the decision was a bit of a dodge and you can bet your bottom dollar that continued legal wrangling about APIs is assuredly going to take place. Legal ramifications of API will resurface again soon enough, mark my words.

The nice thing about discussing APIs is that it provides a moment to reflect on APIs within the legal realm and the advancement of LegalTech.

Say what?

Yes, a very important aspect about the advent of software for law practitioners such as contract management systems, legal case management, and the like is that APIs can come to the fore in that realm too. When considering adopting someone's LegalTech software, a potentially important consideration would be whether they provide APIs for their systems. If they do, it implies that there is a possibility of extending on top of their software, plus there is a chance that other third-party software products will leverage those systems. All in all, it is usually a healthy sign and suggests that the provider is thinking ahead.

For any of you that have perchance used the Harvard Law School Caselaw system, there is a nifty component known as the Caselaw Access Project API (CAPAPI), which allows programmatic access to U.S. court cases published in law books from 1658 to 2018, entailing over six million scanned-in cases.

I mention this as an example of APIs that you perhaps didn't know existed and yet were potentially within your grasp.

A crucial and underway research study by Houman Shadab, Director of the Innovation Center for Law and Technology and a Professor of Law at the New York Law School is closely examining APIs in the development of legal technology (he gave a talk recently at the Stanford *FutureLaw CodeX 2021* conference on his work). He is exploring best practices associated with APIs in LegalTech. The project is being performed as part of the Stanford CodeX Center for Legal Informatics and seeks to showcase how Legal APIs can be devised to benefit the legal community all told.

Conclusion

In my efforts, I've frequently touted the importance of APIs when it comes to advances in AI and the law. Essentially, there will be increased capabilities of tapping into AI-based Legal Reasoning systems (AILRs), doing so by conventional LegalTech that invoke APIs to leverage the budding AILR systems, including law-oriented Machine Learning (ML) and Deep Learning capabilities. For details on this and other AI and law topics, see my book entitled "AI and Legal Reasoning Essentials" (available on Amazon).

I suppose that the next time you go into your kitchen to cook a meal, perhaps you'll be thinking about APIs and SCOTUS, though please don't become so distracted that you end up burning your fine meal of cauliflower steak sauteed with crunchy hazelnuts and a lemon zesty butter sauce. Mulling over APIs isn't worth ruining a well-deserved legal respite and elegant dining experience.

––––––––––

Note: *For supplemental materials depicting the aspects discussed in this chapter, refer to Appendix B, which contains various augmented diagrams, charts, and additional related facets of relevance.*

CHAPTER 11
AI & LAW:
RAMIFICATIONS OF BAD AI

Key briefing points about this article:

- There is much discussion these days about *AI for Good*

- This has startled people into realizing that there is also the potential of *AI for Bad*

- Regulators are considering passing new laws to stem the possibility of Bad AI

- The EU supposedly is considering a severe penalty for firms that promulgate Bad AI

- Attorneys versed in AI and the law are going to find themselves facing a goldmine of work

Introduction

With the rush toward devising AI systems, there was an initial gleeful gushing about how great AI will be and the moniker of *AI for Good* magically came into prominence.

As will be pointed out in a moment, all good things must come to end, as they say, and also the reality is beginning to settle in about whether AI is intrinsically and axiomatically going to be solely for the purposes of good and worthy endeavors. That seems like a rather dubious and unlikely premise.

Meanwhile, please do keep in mind that there isn't any kind of AI as of yet that is sentient, therefore you need to realize that the *AI for Good* is ostensibly about those that develop and field AI systems. If those people responsible for putting together an AI system are aiming to provide a form of automation that is beneficial, and assuming that it indeed produces a beneficial or good outcome, they are presumably doing the right thing and attaining *AI for Good*.

As they say, there is always the other side of a coin. By that account, there is also the *AI for Bad* that can be fostered onto others too.

Once again, do not fall for the mental trap that this is AI that has on its own "decided" to be an evildoer. Humans are working as the Wizard of Oz, doing their wizardry efforts behind the scenes of devising and promulgating their *AI for Bad*, and they rightfully need to be held accountable for their actions. To clarify, they don't necessarily have in their active mind some malevolent thoughts aiming to do bad things. They might unleash an AI system with the best of intentions, and yet the AI is faulty or lacks sufficient guardrails that it subsequently shifts into the *AI for Bad* cauldron.

Some simply denote this as Bad AI.

How might Bad AI be related to lawyers and the practice of law?

Oddly enough, the emergence of Bad AI is going to be altogether a goldmine for lawyers. The basis for such a claim is due to the legal wrangling's that are going to enormously and fervently arise due to Bad AI. Bad AI will stridently push the advent of AI into the legal sphere and therefore those attorneys that are well-prepared have a chance to make a bundle from the burgeoning trend of those that are willy-nilly tossing AI systems into the public arena.

For details on this and other AI and law topics, see my book entitled "AI and Legal Reasoning Essentials" (available on Amazon).

New Regulations About Bad AI

News reports have been stating for a while that the European Union (EU) has been drafting a "Bad AI" piece of legislation that purportedly calls for a financial penalty for companies that unleash non-compliant AI systems. Rumors have been floating endlessly about the potential severity or magnitude of the proposed penalties.

According to recent news reports about a leaked early draft of the "Regulation on a European Approach for Artificial Intelligence," there was supposedly a proposed provision that businesses could be fined up to 4% of their global revenue for having promulgated Bad AI (this was apparently just a proposed provision, but it is seemingly likely there will be some form of eventually mandated sharp-toothed penalties).

The odds are that whatever the EU does, the US is likely to eventually do something of a similar nature. Other countries are bound to follow that same path.

In any case, 4% of annual revenue or any such akin sizable penalty is going to potentially be a quite big chunk of dough. Ergo, the specter of big bucks surrounding those that are (alleged or actual) purveyors of Bad AI means a big opening for attorneys.

You can bet your bottom dollar that when a company is accused of having violated such regulations, they will clamor for versed attorneys that can defend them from the Bad AI accusations and prosecutions. Furthermore, the allegations of fostering Bad AI will be spurred in a herd mentality way, causing a tsunami of such claims to veritably come out of the woodwork. Even firms that have *AI for Good* will undoubtedly get accused of actually generating Bad AI. In some instances, the claim will be utterly false, while in other instances the contention will be potentially valid.

Throughout those matters, astute attorneys that know about the ins and outs of AI and the law will be brought on board to aid in dealing with these substantive considerations.

Eventually, there will be so much of the Bad AI flying around, along with a plethora of accusations about Bad AI being in existence, firms will realize they need to get ahead of the Bad AI game. Businesses will seek out attorneys that can proactively participate in trying to ensure that the AI being produced by a firm will not get summarily blanketed as Bad AI.

Some are saying that if society goes the route of trying to regulate AI as to Bad or Good that this will essentially kill the golden goose. In other words, the societal all-told benefits by providing advances in automation as enabled via AI will be perceived by businesses as not worth the costs. The adverse attention of possibly having let loose Bad AI, along with costly criminal cases or civil lawsuits, will stoke firms to stop making any kind of AI systems.

This seems like a relatively rational form of response. By avoiding anything that might be construed as AI, perhaps the costly gauntlet of getting caught up in Bad AI can be avoided. This certainly on the surface seems indubitably sensible and a prudent notion for all businesses to observe.

Wait for a second, there is yet another twist and it once again ties into attorneys.

As I've mentioned in my prior columns, there is still a great deal of looseness as to the definition of AI and what legally constitutes an AI system. There is a solid chance that whatever regulation is devised about so-called Bad AI will include definitions of AI that you can drive a Mack truck through.

The point is that attorneys will be needed to help ascertain whether a firm demonstrably produced an AI system or not. More work for suitably versed lawyers.

I've saved the most frightening twist for the tail end of this legal tale.

Are you ready?

Suppose a law firm opts to adopt a Bad AI system (let's assume unknowingly so), or perhaps opts to partner or tightly collaborate with a LegalTech firm to produce AI for the legal profession. To what degree will the law firm be considered culpable under any regulation related to Bad AI? It could be that lawyers will need to advise law firms and LegalTech companies about how to keep from affronting the woes of Bad AI.

Conclusion

Overall, despite that last bit of scary news, the primary takeaway is that as AI becomes an increasingly prevalent tech-induced part of our world, there is going to be an increasing need for lawyers with the right acumen about AI and the law to proffer their expertise in this relatively new specialty.

Bad AI might just be good for some attorneys, though I think we would all agree that Bad AI is inherently bad and we aren't wishing for Bad AI, and instead merely wanting to prevent Bad AI from seeing the light of day.

Note: *For supplemental materials depicting the aspects discussed in this chapter, refer to Appendix B, which contains various augmented diagrams, charts, and additional related facets of relevance.*

CHAPTER 12
AI & LAW:
COMPUTABLE CONTRACTS

Key briefing points about this essay:

- Contracts are typically a key element of any legal practice and the work efforts therein

- Computing aids the drafting of legal contracts, albeit somewhat simply so

- Law practices are adopting Contract Lifecycle Management (CLM) tools

- Computable contracts are being advanced via legal scholars and LegalTech vendors

- AI is ultimately an integral component in the future of such contracts

Introduction

Molding clay is an invigorating experience, though it can also have its share of frustration and exasperation.

Perhaps you've perchance molded clay, or at least you've seen others do so. The idea is that you take a raw lump of clay and gradually knead and mold it into whatever kind of object or shape that you are trying to ultimately produce. When attempting to make a clay bowl, you can use your fingers to try and hollow out a boxy bulk of clay and hone the rest from there. Another means to get that desired bowl to emerge would be to use a spinner and shape the clay as it is being rotated.

Have you ever tried to craft a legal contract?

I'm sure that you replied with a resounding yes.

You've likely devised dozens, perhaps hundreds of contracts during your legal career. In a semblance of molding clay, you undoubtedly started with some prior contracts or templates and opted to hone that raw material into the divine contract that you were tasked to create. There are various ways to approach the crafting of a legal contract and we each end up doing so via whatever preferences have been gleaned over the years.

Though some might (still) use paper and pencil, the likelihood is that you used a word processing capability on your computer when composing a contract nowadays. The beauty here is that you can quickly and easily grab passages of contractual text and mesh them together, proceeding to then tweak and sharpen the material. Many law offices have invested in Contract Lifecycle Management (CLM) software to streamline the making, revising, and tracking of contracts as part of their legal practice (for a handy posting on the ROI for CLM, see a recent piece by Lilian Caldeira and Olga Mack entitled "A Quick-Start Guide to CLM Software ROI Calculations" in *Artificial Lawyer*).

Advances in computing are gradually guiding us toward the advent of computable contracts.

Computable Contracts Are Arising

Let's take a look at what that portends.

First, realize that a conventional contract is somewhat like a lump of clay, even after being finished, such that it is not active or proactive in any particular manner. The text just sits there. Humans are needed to examine the contractual language and try to figure out whether the provisions are being lawfully observed. Likewise, humans have to generally be vigilant and stay on top of making sure that if a contract is not abided with, a human-sparked alert about the contractual transgression has to be issued. And so on.

What we need is a proactive variant of contracts that can leverage the computer system and be somewhat vigilant for us (that almost seems anthropomorphic, which is not my intent, namely please do not construe today's computing as somehow sentient).

According to Harry Surden, Professor of Law at the University of Colorado Law School, computable contracts is an emerging and crucial branch of tech and the law: "Contracting parties express their contract in the language of computers – data – which allows the computer to reliably identify the contract components and subjects. The parties also provide the computer with a series of rules that allow the computer to react in a sensible way that is consistent with the underlying meaning of the contractual promises" (in his piece entitled "Computable Contracts Explained" and further expounded in his *UC Davis Law Review* article "Computable Contracts").

One key question is how far along can we expect computable contracts to take us?

Per Surden's additional remarks: "Aren't contracts complex, abstract, and executed in environments of legal and factual uncertainty? Some are, but some aren't. The short answer here is that essentially, the contracts that are made *computable* don't involve the abstract, difficult, or relatively uncertain legal topics that tend to occupy lawyers. Rather (for the moment at least), computers are typically given contract terms and conditions with relatively well-defined subjects and determinable criteria that tend not to involve significant legal or factual uncertainty in the average case."

Efforts to produce computable contracts are being undertaken by devising a Contract Definition Language (CDL), which is akin to a computer programming language but one that is purposely designed to handle the syntax and semantics of contracts. As stated by esteemed Professor Michael Genesereth at Stanford University: "Over the last few years, researchers at CodeX have been working toward the design of a language with these properties. The current leading candidate (called CDL) has three main components – a concept definition language, a legal ontology, and a collection of domain ontologies" (as posted in *Complaw Corner* of the Stanford CodeX Center for Legal Informatics).

Going into further detail, Professor Genesereth noted that: "The legal ontology of CDL is a collection of concepts related to contracts in general – notions such as the meeting of the minds, offer and acceptance, consideration, and so forth. While this ontology is essential for ensuring that contracts are valid, it is unnecessary for determining compliance of situations with the terms and conditions of contracts. For that, we need a domain ontology. A domain ontology consists of words to describe the relevant features of situations."

As I've indicated in my writings about AI and the law, the intertwining of various AI-based techniques and technologies will immensely aid and spur the prevalence of computable contracts (per my column coverage). By applying Machine Learning (ML), Deep Learning (DL), and Natural Language Processing (NLP), you can anticipate that contracts will be computationally analyzed and fostered into being proactive. For details on this and other AI and law topics, see my book entitled "AI and Legal Reasoning Essentials" (available on Amazon).

Contracts are what makes the world go round, some would vigorously assert.

Conclusion

You might recall from your contract's classes in law school about the infamous case of the man that tried to compel Pepsi to provide him with a Harrier jet due to having collected and submitted seven million Pepsi Points as based on a popular Pepsi promotional ad campaign (see the delightful analysis of the case as propounded in the *Nevada Law Journal* by Keith Rowley, Professor of Law, University of Nevada Las Vegas). Despite outsized arguments that Pepsi had ostensibly proffered a valid offer, the court ultimately ruled via extended logic that the matter did not rise to be construed as a contract and was most clearly tendered in jest.

I think most of us would agree that contracts are no laughing matter. The future of contracts is inexorably going to encompass computable contracts, along with a marriage of AI capabilities, out of which you can expect some ironclad benefits for the legal profession.

———

Note: *For supplemental materials depicting the aspects discussed in this chapter, refer to Appendix B, which contains various augmented diagrams, charts, and additional related facets of relevance.*

CHAPTER 13

AI & LAW:

C-SUITE BUY-IN

Key briefing points about this article:

- Most companies require C-suite buy-in or approval for the by-function budget requests

- As a longtime CIO/CTO, I've worked hand-in-hand with Chief Legal Officers (CLOs)

- Trying to get the C-suite to spend toward LegalTech has been an ongoing uphill battle

- A recent EY Law and Harvard Law School survey showcases those difficulties

- Leveraging and in a sense exploiting AI-based LegalTech can inure a budgetary buy-in

Introduction

Do you like those classic show-tunes and songs that make your heart sing?

I hope so.

Here's a line that might bring a smile to your face and give you a moment to step aside from your daily pressures. A spoonful of sugar makes the medicine go down. Yes, the medicine goes down, the medicine goes down.

We all know that popular wording and the heartwarming sentiment it carries.

The outsized and cheerfully famous tune is likely to start swirling in your head by the mere mention of those ever so delightful words. Part of the reason that the catchphrase is amazingly memorable and semantically powerful could be due to the sensibility and abject succinctness in revealing an altogether human truth. Namely, we tend to not want to take our medicine, even though it would possibly cure our ills, and sometimes a dose of sugar provides a dollop of sweetness to overcome the sour-tasting prescribed treatment.

Hang onto that thought and allow the song to percolate in your mind as you see where I'm taking you. You are about to go on a journey into the realm of in-house legal counsel budgets and the ever-present gut-wrenching gauntlet to get funding for the pressing legal matters of a firm.

Having been a longtime CIO/CTO and worked hand-in-hand with many Chief Legal Officers (CLOs), I know firsthand how hard it can be to get the rest of the C-suite to understand and approve our annual funding requests for the legal teams. Such requests usually encompass the various computers and essential tech that are needed to properly run, lead, and operate the legal side of the house. Sadly, oftentimes the legal beagles are the last to get modern IT equipment and are left to fend for themselves. Without the right hardware and software, the legal team is forced into doing manual tasks that are unproductive and ostensibly wastes the prized labor of those highly versed legal professionals.

For those of you that had done battle with your C-suite on such matters, you are probably not going to be especially surprised at the results of a recent survey about the woes and constraints facing in-house legal budgetary aspects.

Though this might not be shocking news, it nonetheless helps to give you strength that you are not alone and that your peers are faced with the same kinds of frustrations and roadblocks as you are.

A survey undertaken by EY Law and the Harvard Law School indicated that 70% of in-house legal teams do not have adequate technology and that the biggest hurdle toward overcoming the stark disparity entails convincing the C-suite that something substantive needs to be done. In a sense, you could assert that the buck stops at the C-suite table. When it comes to slicing up the corporate pie and garnering funding for each of the functions of the firm there is a regrettable and ongoing tradition of starving the legal teams.

EY Global Law co-leader Cornelius Grossmann was quoted as stating that "As the world starts to move toward economic recovery, enabling growth will be a crucial priority for organizations all over the world. If organizations are to thrive and businesses are to remain compliant, law, procurement, and commercial contracting departments will need to ensure they are ready to face an ever-growing list of regulatory risks."

The survey respondents were nearly unanimous on this key insight: A whopping 97% said that they found themselves struggling to get investments approved for buying, fielding, and keeping up-to-date their LegalTech. LegalTech is an umbrella term used to refer to all kinds of computer-based legal systems and technology required to efficiently and effectively perform the legal affairs of the company.

Using The Triumphant Banner Of AI-Based LegalTech

And this brings us to the earlier stated wisdom that a spoonful of sugar can make the medicine go down. I trust that the tune is still rattling around in your noggin and that you hadn't forgotten my promise to bring us back to that stirring topic.

Here's what I mean.

Let's start by discussing two kinds of LegalTech.

There is the conventional LegalTech that has what I might refer to as making use of conventional technology and leverages tried-and-true hardware and software. The other type of LegalTech is the type that has been augmented with Artificial Intelligence (AI) capabilities. This is AI-based LegalTech or some prefer to call it AI-augmented LegalTech (I'll use those phrasings interchangeably and proffer no particular preference in the naming), which stretches the boundaries beyond the injection of conventional technology.

Before I get further into this discussion, please know that the AI elements are not at all sentient, and anyone making such claims should be entirely disbelieved and I would argue they should be pursued for their false and misleading statements. I've repeatedly tried to rein in those overstated and wrongly formulated exaggerations and hyperbolic contentions. For my down-to-earth details on this and other AI and law topics, see my book entitled "AI and Legal Reasoning Essentials" (available on Amazon).

Depending upon the AI used to augment LegalTech, this can result in an infusion that demonstrably improves the LegalTech and makes it a much better choice than conventional LegalTech. Be forewarned that this positive outcome is not always the case. Lamentably, some are tossing AI at LegalTech and hoping that it sticks. Those wanton attempts are unfortunate and tend to give a blackeye to other AI-based LegalTech efforts.

Bottom-line is this: *The AI added to LegalTech can become the spoonful of sugar that gets the C-suite to take their medicine and like it.*

In other words, today's C-suite tends to be relatively convinced that they need to do something with and about AI. They usually aren't sure what AI is, nor what they should do about it. But that doesn't matter per se in this context, since we can simply leverage the prevailing cachet about AI and marry it to the need to get funding for the legal teams in terms of their LegalTech requirements.

By reorienting the legal team budget requests and emphasizing the AI-based LegalTech, you can attract the attention of the C-suite. I'd argue that the AI stuff is indeed more than just sugar, providing added value, and meanwhile, it does have a sugary semblance in today's AI-obsessed society. The highlighting of the AI-based LegalTech in the request can provide a twofer. It will potentially get you the right kind of LegalTech and it will get the C-suite to approve the request.

Conclusion

If that seems like a sneaky ploy, you might want to consider that many of the other heads of the other functions are all trying the same scheme. In that manner, you are merely fighting fire with fire. Or, do you want to be the only one unarmed and sitting there in dismay as once again your LegalTech budgetary lines get axed.

You'll need to make that decision and let the AI chips fall where they may.

Note: *For supplemental materials depicting the aspects discussed in this chapter, refer to Appendix B, which contains various augmented diagrams, charts, and additional related facets of relevance.*

CHAPTER 14

AI & LAW:
STANDARDS FOR LEGALTECH

Key briefing points about this essay:

- Worldwide shipping is a marvel partially due to the advent of shipping container standards

- By establishing standards for sizes of shipping containers the global shipping effort eased

- In the legal field, there are nascent standards such as the well-known LEDES for billing

- Other new standards are being formed such as for NDAs, contracts, and the like

- It is time to forge forward on standards for the AI aspects of the legal field and LegalTech

Introduction

You likely are unaware of the importance that standards play in your life. There is little immediate attention usually paid toward standards. We take them for granted.

That being said, you might be somewhat surprised or at least pleasantly startled to know that standards are what makes the world go round. In particular, the primary reason that we have such efficient and effective worldwide shipping today can be attributed to the advent of a very important and altogether seemingly simple standard. That standard has to do with the size of shipping containers.

It used to be that shipping containers varied tremendously in their length, width, and height. This was a sorrowful state of affairs. The oddball sizes and shapes meant that trucks intending to haul shipping containers could not do a one-size-fits-all approach to trucking. Instead, there was a bewildering array of issues that varied per each idiosyncratic sizing choice. It was also difficult to stack containers since they would not readily fit on top of each other.

Cranes at shipping docks had to deal with the quirky sizes. Some shipping ports would only take certain sizes, thus you had to logistically make sure that the right sized container got trucked to the right particular shipping port. Ships that were tasked with carrying the vaunted shipping containers were unable to readily pack the containers on board and the amount of time devoted to loading and unloading the bulky and uneven containers meant that ships had to waste time sitting in ports versus moving the goods across the open seas.

After realizing that the situation was quite a mess, there was a herculean effort to get everybody to agree to a set standard for shipping containers. You can imagine the infighting that took place. Some wanted one size, others wanted a different size. It all depended upon what kinds of trucks, ships, or cranes that you already had in hand. Eventually, this roadblock toward attaining a universal sizing criterion was overcome.

Today, we can thank that globally adopted standard for the ease in which worldwide shipping occurs. Shipping of containers is a relatively seamless process nowadays (in terms of the types of potential containers and their capacities). Trucks are prepared to handle the standard sizes.

Cranes handle the standard sizes. Ships are built to appropriately cart the standard sizes. Costs for shipping came down, ease of shipping went up, and the shipping industry is a thriving economic engine that brings to you just about everything you currently own or use.

I'm guessing that you are now presumably convinced that standards can be a boon and ought to assuredly be stridently put in place where appropriate to do so.

Standards And The Field Of Law

You might be wondering, what does that have to do with the field of law?

Let's specifically focus our attention on the use of technology in the legal profession. The typical way to refer to such technology is to call it LegalTech. LegalTech is an umbrella term used to refer to all kinds of computer-based legal systems and other high-tech that aid everyday legal activities and can demonstrably boost performance when proffering legal services.

When applying tech to other fields of endeavor, such as in the medical domain or so-called MedTech, there are various standards associated with the field of medicine. You could say that they have already figured out their shipping container problem and generally resolved it (well, not entirely, but you get the gist).

The LegalTech field is a far cry from having any of the substantive needed standards that would put it on par with other fields like MedTech. We are faced with a shipping container dilemma and it is getting pretty much worse with each passing day.

That being said, please know that there are valiant efforts underway to identify, define, and promulgate standards in the legal field that will greatly hasten further advances in LegalTech. For example, the longtime standard known as Legal Electronic Data Exchange Standard (LEDES) has done a lot to promote the commonality and interfacing between legal-oriented computer apps encompassing billing for legal services.

Over the years, the LEDES has been gradually enhanced to allow for more code sets, customized fields, etc.

Similar to the idea of aligning trucks, shipping ports, and ships, the LEDES has helped align how legal pros categorize their time and legal services, along with enabling the streamlining of legal software and legal databases to share billing data accordingly. Achieved merely by agreeing (in a sense) to a standardized notion of length, width, and height.

There is also the Legal Matter Standard Specification (LMSS) that has been created via the Standards Advancement for the Legal Industry (SALI) non-profit alliance. As stated by SALI, this is a crucial taxonomy of legal services that can be used "when implementing workflows, business intelligence systems or machine learning systems."

Richard Tromans at the *Artificial Lawyer* has pointed out that a newly launched Legal Standards Database is taking shape, covering emerging standards such as OneNDA for a universal NDA or non-disclosure agreement template, the ISDA for standards regarding contract clauses, the Legal Schema that focuses on structured data in contracts, and so on. These will be instrumental in dealing with the infamous shipping container problem as it pertains to LegalTech.

There is another facet of LegalTech that will also need to have suitable standards established, namely in the Artificial Intelligence (AI) aspects as integrated into LegalTech. For my coverage on this and other AI and law topics, see my book entitled "AI and Legal Reasoning Essentials" (available on Amazon).

In brief, we need to agree on setting standards for legal-oriented knowledge representation, legal-based knowledge reasoning, UX or user-experience interface aspects in an AI and lawyering context (especially dealing with Natural Language Processing or NLP), and also for APIs (application programming interfaces) involved in activating legal-oriented AI and machine learning computational components.

If we are going to have AI-based systems in the legal field, ostensibly being able to assist or potentially perform legal advisory services, the best way to proceed entails agreeing to a set of standards. Right now, most of the AI-enablement efforts are being done in disparate ways and there is no ready means to pair up one AI-augmented LegalTech with another.

They don't get along in the sense that they are each doing things their own computationally idiosyncratic way.

Conclusion

The next time that you see a truck hauling a shipping container, think about how standards play a hidden and yet vital role in getting the hauled goods from point A to point B. We want AI to also get us from point A to point B in the tendering of legal services. It will be a nightmare to do so if we allow dissimilar approaches to limit the pace and scalability underlying AI-based Legal Reasoning (AILR) systems.

Time to join together and get some measured liftoff for those budding AI-based LegalTech capabilities.

.

Note: *For supplemental materials depicting the aspects discussed in this chapter, refer to Appendix B, which contains various augmented diagrams, charts, and additional related facets of relevance.*

Dr. Lance B. Eliot

CHAPTER 15
AI & LAW:
NO CODE

Key briefing points about this essay:

- Lawyers and the legal profession are nowadays discussing code aplenty

- There is the notion of law-as-code

- There is the case made by some that lawyers ought to be coders

- A differing view asserts that lawyers should be using no-code toolsets

- The bottom-line about no-code is to do your homework and keep your eyes open

Introduction

Lawyers and the legal profession are keenly talking about and wringing their hands over the topic of code.

Nearly any law industry conference, webinar, seminar, event, or legal news publication will inescapably have something to say about code.

Let's explore what that's about.

Many pundits tout the idea that the law itself is ostensibly code (i.e., akin to the "code" or program coding that is devised for computers) and therefore we need to rethink the fundamental nature of how our laws are written and implemented (I've covered this topic in prior columns, take a look).

Another code-related perspective is that lawyers need to know how to write programming code and ergo shift their attention away from the usual drudgery of proffering legal advice. The future for savvy attorneys is said to be filled with riches if they would merely refocus their efforts and become proficient at writing code. That is the *lawyers-as-coders* camp (this has been covered in my prior columns, which you might want to glance at).

There is an additional camp that has gradually become the elephant in the room or perhaps the 600-pound gorilla, namely the aspiration of attaining the venerated *no-code* capability for lawyers that want to do tech things.

The belief or best hope would be to avoid entirely the by-hand labor intensive and specialized skillset of being a coder or computer programmer or software engineer. Instead, a lawyer could be, well, a lawyer, and somehow cause code to be generated for whatever online or computer-based task they wish to undertake. This takes that whole lawyer-as-coders question and tosses it out the window. The no-code approach is posited on the notion that you can otherwise do coding without having to be a coder.

Let the computer do the coding for you.

I realize that a smarmy attorney might argue that even if a lawyer is not actually directly writing code per se, yet if they are nonetheless somehow generating or producing code, it would seem like you could still paint them with the lawyer-as-coder label. Believe it or not, despite that seemingly obtuse or silly argumentative posture, you'll see in a moment that there is a kernel of truth therein.

Anyway, we shall begin by exploring what this no-code or sometimes referred to as so-called *zero coding* is all about. It would be helpful to first establish what conventional coding consists of. Perhaps when you were in college, you might have taken a beginner's programming class and used something like the BASIC programming language, or in more modern times the choice is often Python or Java. If you've never done that type of computer coding, at least you've likely written a macro or two while using spreadsheet software.

One way or another, you seemingly must know that coding generally involves writing a series of statements in a prescribed computer programming language. To do so, you need to know what the programming language allows and how to properly write code in that language. You then write statements that end up instructing the computer to do various things such as calculating values or printing out a report. Of course, we all also know that at times a coded program goes afoul and might contain errors in logic or other problems. Dealing with those issues usually involves debugging the code.

Suppose you could avoid learning a programming language and in lieu have the computer generate the code on your behalf. For example, you might use some kind of visual interface having a drag-and-drop look-and-feel that allows you to easily assemble elements that you want to have performed. Click on a Lego-like construct that will do some handy equation calculations and drag this capability into your budding "program" that will figure out the total of your billable hours for the month.

That is the way that most of the no-code systems work. They usually present a graphical interface and let you devise a program in a flowcharting manner. You then use a menu item to generate and execute or perform the generated code.

You don't need to see the code and can usually take it for granted that code was produced (this is a technical simplification, done for brevity herein).

Those NCDP's Are Arising

A rash of NCDP's (No Code Development Platforms) has come into the legal marketplace. These are no-code facilities that are purposely oriented and tailored toward legal tasks and are intended for legal professions such as lawyers to use, aiming at coding related to legal contracts, legal case writing, etc.

Keep in mind that there are NCDPs for generic programming, unrelated to legal tasks, and also that there are other customizations of NCDPs for other domains, such as for financial specialists that want to do no-code work.

Do these no-code efforts succeed?

As they say, your mileage will vary.

It could be that a no-code for legal tasks might be handy if you also realize the constraints that such systems usually have. To a certain degree, you can be hampered while trying to do a full-bodied semblance of "programming" and will be confined to whatever the tool has been devised to allow.

There is the other nagging concern that you are potentially using lawyers to once again be doing a variant of coding. Wait for a second, you might exclaim, the no-code seems to promise that an attorney isn't doing any coding.

That's where the rub comes in. The argument goes that coding is more than the mere writing of programming statements. A true computer programmer/analyst or software engineer needs to consider what the requirements are for the task being programmed, they need to develop the code, debug the code, and field the resultant program. That is considered the system development life cycle.

A lawyer that uses a no-code tool is either unaware that they are immersing themselves into a system's development life cycle, or they are purposely ignoring it. A concern is then raised about how robust the resulting "coded capability" is going to be and whether it might be duplicative of other capabilities that already exist. In short, a company fostering lawyers that use no-code might find itself gradually drenched in tons of these no-code mini-programs and for which they are a scattering and disconnected plate of spaghetti.

The desire to avoid bottlenecks of the IT function of the firm can inadvertently produce a mess and turn a clean portfolio of apps into a multi-headed monster. There are concerns too about ensuring proper computer security considerations are taken into account for the plethora of no-code mini-programs being shared around the office.

Overall, the no-code is not an assured cure-all. There are gotchas involved. That being said, upcoming improvements in no-code systems by infusing AI will help tremendously. For my coverage on this and other AI and law topics, see my book entitled "AI and Legal Reasoning Essentials" (available on Amazon).

Conclusion

Like most things in life, the no-code ambition is certainly worthwhile, but you need to do your homework and due diligence, making sure that any no-code for legal tasks will aid your legal beagles and not get them and nor your law firm into a troubling no-code abyss.

Note: *For supplemental materials depicting the aspects discussed in this chapter, refer to Appendix B, which contains various augmented diagrams, charts, and additional related facets of relevance.*

CHAPTER 16

AI & LAW:
HUMAN SIGNS OF DISHONESTY

Key briefing points about this essay:

- Robot judges continue to be a topic of keen discussion and at times heated debate

- A disturbing and misleading trend aims to say that robot judges can detect dishonesty

- Predictions are that robot judges will use sensors to assess body language and human signs

- This seems somehow glorious but is outstretched and misguided

- Time to set the record straight and make sure that robot judges are aiming correctly

Introduction

A whole lot of discussion and at times heated debate keeps arising about robot judges.

I'm referring to the possibility of having Artificial Intelligence (AI) that can serve in the capacity of a courtroom judge. This might be done in a physical manifestation entailing a robot that walks and talks or could be done more subtly by an AI-based system that resembles an everyday computer such as a laptop or smartphone sitting on a desk. The "robot" part of the catchphrase tends to jar us into believing that robot judges will look like human judges, but that is not necessarily a requirement for AI-based adjudication.

Will robot judges be good or bad for humanity?

Glad you asked.

Robot judges seem to either be heralded as the judicial hero that will ensure abject fairness and remove the bane of human biases from today's adjudication, or they are the worst idea ever and will be nothing more than emotionless calculating machines that make heartless decisions impacting people's lives. It is assuredly confounding as to which way things are going to ultimately end up.

There's another twist involving robot judges that keeps getting attention and for which regrettably is garnering undue credence. I hope that the somewhat trending topic will eventually be cast aside as an altogether ridiculous notion and unworthy of further focus.

I'm referring to the posited conjecture that robot judges will summarily be able to perform their acts of deciding upon guilt versus innocence by the simple and seemingly straightforward means of gauging the outward appearances of human dishonesty.

Allow me to explain. Some pundits are claiming that those AI-based robot judges will be using sensory devices such as video cameras and audio microphones to look at and hear what is said by any accused defendant in court. Just as facial recognition technology has been utilized to try and ascertain whether someone is happy or sad, angry or calm, and so on, the idea is that the robot judge can amazingly examine numerous facets of human behavior and ergo conclusively figure out whether someone is guilty or not.

The AI will assess the body language of the subject.

A slew of detection activities will be undertaken in the courtroom. Is the defendant fidgety? What kinds of gestures is the person making with their hands and arms? Do the eyes of the defendant dart fervently? In addition to those kinds of detections, the robot judge would be armed with thermal imaging sensors and could measure the body temperature and similar physical elements such as pulse rate, etc.

Presumably, the AI will have been prior trained via advances in Machine Learning (ML) and Deep Learning (DL) to match the detectable characteristics to those of "known" guilty parties in some form of collected training database. As a clarification, ML/DL is a computational pattern matching technique and statistically tries to pick up patterns in a trove of data, which can then reuse the discovered patterns when shown a new instance.

There is nothing magical about this latest form of AI and please do not be taken in by charlatans that suggest we have reached a level of machine-based sentience. Not so. Not even close. I've repeatedly tried to rein in those overstated and wrongly formulated exaggerations and hyperbolic contentions. For my down-to-earth details on this and other AI and law topics, see my book entitled "AI and Legal Reasoning Essentials" (available on Amazon).

Anyway, the brash assertion that is being proffered these days is that a robot judge will be able to determine whether someone is lying and do so with a claimed 99.9% accuracy level. By interpreting the physical signs of human behavior that supposedly reveal dishonesty, the robot judge can grandly declare the person to be guilty or innocent.

Furthermore, the same outrageous claim adds that these types of human tells or cues would generally be imperceptible to human judges. In that manner of relief, this implies that robot judges could do a decidedly better job at judging than could human judges. Human judges are apparently insufficient at and inadequate for being able to sense and include the myriad of non-verbal and also verbal signals of liars versus truth-tellers.

I mean, why even have trials at all?

Bring the accused into a room where a robot judge has been seated. Have the person make their case. One supposes that attorneys aren't needed and the whole shebang can be settled within a few minutes of observation by the robot judge.

Case closed.

One especially prominent prediction made last year was that roughly fifty years hence from now (by the year 2070), there will be robot judges just like this that will have stridently been put in place, and the world will find itself commonly having robot judges dispensing daily decisions entailing justice in a nearly "error-free" manner. Fewer instances of falsely decided guilt, and more instances of rightfully ascertained guilt.

Indeed, the robot judges will be doing so well that we can replace human judges almost entirely and no longer be undermined by the biases and foibles of those (ugh!) human decision-makers.

Let's Not Have Those Kinds Of Robot Judges

The breathless enthusiasm for this outstretched approach is not just misguided, it is abundantly scary and quite an abomination.

First, the equating of a semblance of dishonesty with the weighty matter of guilt in a given case is absurd on the face of it all. A person might appear to be dishonest, though this has no bearing on the judicial question at hand. Also, some people can appear to be dishonest by the measures suggested, and yet be entirely honest and only exhibiting alleged signs of dishonesty.

Second, what has happened to constitutional concerns about self-incrimination? Apparently, the future entailing robot judges also necessitates tossing out the constitutional right to not give testimony against oneself, and for which this intrusive sensory battery appears to be so doing.

Third, the vital criterion of intent seems to have gotten lost between now and this Utopian (Dystopian?) future. I concur with the remarks of Phil Lindan in his piece "Can AI Let Justice Be Done?" that crisply stated: "In common-law systems, a crime is committed when a guilty act is perpetrated by a person with a 'guilty mind' or *mens rea*. So, part of what is going on in a criminal court, and in the mind of the jurors, is an attempt to answer the question of the state of mind of a defendant" (*The Gradient*, January 29, 2021).

The list of issues and problems associated with the robot judge as a dishonesty-detection mechanism is nearly endless. Would people sneakily get trained on how to control their physical actions to try and fool the robot judges? What about people that perhaps naturally are adept at controlling themselves and can natively fool the sensory detection? And so on.

All told, hanging one's hat on a hanging judge that does the job by mere detection of human signs of dishonesty is nonsensical and ought to be hung up. In the end, hopefully, this notion will be discarded and fail to gain any traction.

Conclusion

The thing is, this kind of false imagery or bogus vision of robot judges is going to dampen the true interest and value of AI-based judge-related systems, and that's a darned shame. There are numerous ways that a robot judge could augment human judges. There is even the possibility of autonomous robot judges that do not require human judges. We might lose momentum toward devising appropriate AI-based robot judges by having to contend with nonsense claims and crummy distortions. Sadly, the fad of seeking the all-knowing sensory-based dishonesty-detecting robot judge is going to give robot judges a bad name. Poor robot judges, they just can't get any respect.

———————

Note: *For supplemental materials depicting the aspects discussed in this chapter, refer to Appendix B, which contains various augmented diagrams, charts, and additional related facets of relevance.*

CHAPTER 17

AI & LAW:
SOFT LAW ON AI

Key briefing points about this essay:

- Soft law is oftentimes a precursor to officially formalized hard laws

- The arising of soft law tends to occur when shoring up new domains or innovations

- A slew of soft law has emerged in the burgeoning field of AI

- Arizona State University (ASU) College of Law has established a database of soft law about AI

- This database is a veritable treasure trove, publicly available, and can be sliced-and-diced

Introduction

Some would contend that there is the law and then there is everything else. You've likely heard that well-worn line before. It is certainly eye-catching and memorable.

What makes the catchphrase especially interesting is that somewhere in that morass is so-called soft law, sitting somewhat in a no man's zone. Yes, there is a nebulous grey area that is not quite a law and yet oftentimes provides a law-like shaping and tonal directive toward what we can do, including whether our actions are seemingly lawful or ostensibly could veer into becoming unlawful. This mushy realm is commonly known as soft law.

It is said that soft law at times provides the seeds for the formation of future on-the-books laws. In a sense, soft law is floated around and if it gets enough traction then the odds are that official regulations and more formal law will be enacted based on those tried out precepts.

The malleability of soft law is a great strength and simultaneously a potential weakness. As a strength, soft laws can be changed and refined readily. No big hassle, no need to jump through a lot of arduous hoops. Adjustments can be made, remade, and altered time and again. You could argue that this is a big plus since soft law can iteratively be improved until it is finally ripened to be turned into conventional law.

A downside is that all that malleability means that there is something amorphous and intangible about soft law. You cannot stake all your eggs on the soft law since at any time it can be revised, revamped, or entirely reimagined. That is a bit of a slippery slope to depend upon.

One of the most frequent growth patterns of soft law entails domains that are new to the conventional forces of law. If there are scant on-the-books laws in the legal basket about a new domain then the advent of soft law can rush in to momentarily bolster the fresh ground. Rather than waiting for the mainstay of law to catch up with a rapidly advancing innovation, soft law speedily emerges as a stopgap to signal what might be coming down the pike later on.

Soft Law About AI

What innovation or domain comes to mind as a key exemplar of this soft law burgeoning appearance?

A somewhat new innovation that has garnered a tsunami of soft law is the modern-day emergence of Artificial Intelligence (AI) as evidenced by the myriad of AI-based apps and AI-infused computer systems that keep being unleashed. They are seemingly everywhere. And you can bet your bottom dollar that the wild crush of more AI is going to steam ahead, relatively unabated.

There are two ways to think about the law and AI.

I'll briefly highlight the two approaches herein. For my detailed analyses on this and other AI and law topics, see my book entitled "AI and Legal Reasoning Essentials" (available on Amazon).

One approach is to consider how the law ought to govern or regulate the development, testing, and fielding of AI systems. Some fervently contend that existing laws are insufficient to handle what today's AI is bringing to the world, including qualms about embedded biases and other maladies.

The second approach involves applying AI to the law, potentially automating aspects of the law such as being able to computationally undertake legal reasoning. An overarching goal for many entails someday producing autonomous AI systems that can perform legal services on par with human lawyers. That's the famous or perhaps infamous lawyer-in-a-box efforts that are energetically arising in the LegalTech marketplace.

We will focus this specific discussion on the first approach, dealing with laws that govern the advent of AI.

In a manner of consideration, you could point out that the governance of the AI system is also applicable to the second approach, wherein we ostensibly need laws to aid in governing the application of AI to the law and aim to ensure that AI Legal Reasoning (AILR) is purposefully overseen.

As mentioned, many emphasize that existing laws are inadequate when it comes to overseeing and regulating the AI tidal wave.

A newly released collection covering soft law about AI has become available and I would earnestly applaud this as a sorely needed and altogether handy treasure trove, especially since it is publicly accessible for all to see and leverage. Esteemed colleagues Carlos Ignacio Gutierrez and Gary Marchant at Arizona State University (ASU) College of Law have made a herculean effort to put together this amazing database (which can be accessed at https://lsi.asulaw.org/softlaw/ along with research papers describing the collection, and heartily acknowledges the many ASU law students that aided in the compilation and screening process).

Their jointly co-authored paper states this about the work: "Soft law is defined as a program that sets substantive expectations, but is not directly enforceable by government. Because soft law is not bound by a geographic jurisdiction and can be developed, amended, and adopted by any entity, it will be the dominant form of artificial intelligence (AI) governance for the foreseeable future. The objective of this document is to compile and analyze global trends on how this governance tool is used by government, non-profits, and the private sector to manage AI's methods and applications."

A resultant database in a spreadsheet is posted online and contains information about a wide array of soft law AI initiatives. You can easily slice-and-dice the database via the spreadsheet, such as grouping by country of origin, type of entity, and the like. There are over 600 soft law AI efforts listed. The researchers also sought to categorize the set by various themes and sub-themes: "One of the original contributions of this research is its classification of each program's text. By harnessing our 15 themes and 78 sub-themes, we uncovered that general mentions of transparency, general mentions of discrimination and bias, and AI literacy are the most represented issues in our database."

Anyone interested in soft law about AI, and that is trying to garner too what formal regulations might eventually look like, should peruse this collection. Per the existing need to try and rein in the AI out-of-control spiral of *AI For Bad* (meaning adverse outcomes as sparked by AI systems), soft law is trying desperately to curtail the numerous bad apples in the barrel.

Conclusion

As a final remark, for now, the researchers make this poignant indication: "Soft law is not a panacea or silver bullet. By itself, it is unable to solve all of the governance issues experienced by society due to AI. Nevertheless, whether by choice or necessity, soft law is and will continue to play a central role in the governance of AI for some time."

That is a keen insight and showcases that sometimes soft law is the only sheriff in town, while the rest of the troops are gradually, slowly, painstakingly getting formed up.

.

Note: *For supplemental materials depicting the aspects discussed in this chapter, refer to Appendix B, which contains various augmented diagrams, charts, and additional related facets of relevance.*

CHAPTER 18

AI & LAW:
REGULATING AI

Key briefing points about this essay:

- AI systems keep being developed and fielded by the thousands upon thousands

- Some liken this to the days of the wild west, whereby existing laws are deficient

- As a result, many AI systems seem lawless or sneakily skirt the law

- Proposals exist about shoring up existing laws to make sure that AI gets reined in

- Consider a set of legal principles regarding AI that The Alan Turing Institute proposes

Introduction

AI systems are popping up aplenty.

You've undoubtedly seen or heard via daily news reports about those breathtaking new "miraculous" AI systems being put into use all around us.

Seemingly zillions of AI-infused apps are being unleashed. Let's be clear that these are not the type of sci-fi-style AI that you've seen wildly portrayed in movies and TV shows. Instead, these are quite humdrum in comparison. And yet they bode for some sour results and are demonstratively disconcerting without necessarily having to be the caliber of AI that takes over and somehow entirely subjugates humanity.

These ostensibly mundane AI systems of today have already at times crossed over the line on inappropriateness and chillingly showcased unsettling problems. For example, serious qualms about AI systems that are supposed to aid our courts in ascertaining crucial aspects such as bail, sentences, and the nature of parole have been raised. Rightfully so since some of those AI-augmented computer systems contain underlying algorithms and pattern matching techniques that silently embed undue biases and improper profiling.

Many are calling for added governance over AI.

The belief and genuine concern are that our existing laws are not sufficient to rein in the freewheeling AI-apps proliferation steamroller. Greater regulatory oversight is needed to adequately ensure that AI systems are developed and fielded in a manner that respects human beings and our human rights. The myriad of AI developers and entities deploying AI systems have to become cognizant that they need to rigorously and with abject responsibility adhere to fundamental civil and social rights.

For my coverage on this and other AI and law topics, see my book entitled "AI and Legal Reasoning Essentials" available on Amazon.

You might be wondering what do our laws need to contain if they are currently deemed as insufficient when it comes to overseeing AI applications.

A Strawman List Of Legal Precepts Covering AI

A recent in-depth analysis by the Public Policy Programme of The Alan Turing Institute entitled "Artificial Intelligence, Human Rights, Democracy, And The Rule Of Law: A Primer" lays out a useful indication of where our laws seem deficient. In addition, and perhaps most importantly, a set of principles and priorities for a legal framework covering AI systems is included in the insightful work co-authored by researchers David Leslie, Christopher Burr, Mhairi Aitken, Josh Cowls, Mike Katell, and Morgan Briggs.

Let's take a brief look at each of the nine precepts that they maintain are necessary to embody in modern-day laws and that ergo would adequately encompass the advent of AI. I'm paraphrasing the contents of the principles to highlight the main points covered:

- **Human Dignity:** AI systems need to treat humans as moral subjects, rather than as mere objects to be algorithmically scored or manipulated.

- **Human Freedom and Autonomy:** AI systems should be designed and devised to serve as enrichment for humans and not be utilized to condition or control humanity.

- **Prevention Of Harm:** AI cannot be allowed to adversely impact the wellbeing of humans and nor undercut planetary health. Safeguards must be intrinsically encompassed into AI systems accordingly.

- **Non-Discrimination, Gender Equality, Fairness, and Diversity:** AI systems have to exhibit fairness, equity, and inclusiveness in their beneficial impacts. The right to non-discrimination, equity and equality, and equal treatment under the law must be baked solidly and integrally into AI applications.

- **Transparency and Explainability of AI Systems:** AI that is used as part of any product or service must provide a capability to explain the rationale underlying the actions and outputs of the system, doing so especially for the individuals directly affected by the AI application.

- **Data Protection and the Right To Privacy:** Humans have the right to control their personal data and thusly AI systems must properly secure a person's right to protect this data. Such AI applications are to ensure that consent is unambiguously provided, freely given, and based on being effectively informed.

- **Accountability and Responsibility:** Remedies to redress harms caused by AI systems must be available and accessible to those so affected. Furthermore, persons that devise and deploy AI systems must be held accountable when legal norms are violated and when harm occurs.

- **Democracy:** AI systems must not undercut democracy, and indeed have a duty to ensure that democratic decision-making processes are transparent and inclusive. There must be provisions to safeguard pluralism, autonomy, and the economic and social rights of humans.

- **Rule of Law:** Judicial independence, due process, and impartiality must not be undermined by AI systems.

As stated by this venerated primer, these precepts are considered a wide-angled view of the law: "These nine principles and priorities are horizontally applicable. They apply to the design, development, and deployment of AI systems across sectors and use cases, though they could be combined with a sector-specific approach that provides (more detailed) contextual requirements in the form of soft law instruments, such as sectoral standards, guidelines, or assessment lists."

Conclusion

Lawyers need to be mindful that existing laws might not satisfactorily cover the nuances that AI-based systems bring to the world at large. You can expect that our laws will assuredly be modified and possibly written anew to try and encompass the concerns about how AI is being derived and fostered onto an unsuspecting public. Regulators and our courts are bound to find themselves dragged into these machinations, whether they like it or not, and those attorneys that opt to specialize in the realm of AI and the law are likely to find themselves at the forefront of what is yet to come.

All are welcome to this venerable new club and commended for aiding in shaping the future of where AI will go.

.

––––––––––

Note: *For supplemental materials depicting the aspects discussed in this chapter, refer to Appendix B, which contains various augmented diagrams, charts, and additional related facets of relevance.*

Dr. Lance B. Eliot

CHAPTER 19

AI & LAW:

PRIMER ON AI AND LAW

Key briefing points about this essay:

- There is some confusion about what "AI and the law" constitutes

- Some see only a part of the whole and become focused solely on a particular piece

- Thus it is useful to take a holistic look at the entirety of AI and the law

- This quick primer depicts a two-way street framework

- In short, there is: (1) AI applied to the law, and (2) Law applied to AI

Introduction

Sometimes it is hard to see the big picture.

There is much discussion about AI and the law, oftentimes occurring in somewhat fragmented ways. This can especially occur when mired in the details.

It is the proverbial seeing of the trees and not grasping the entirety of the forest. Let's consider taking a look at the forest for the trees, doing so in the case of AI and the law.

Turns out that any confusion or misconceptions about AI and the law can readily be put to bed since the whole phenomena can be relatively directly defined, as will be covered briefly herein.

First, it perhaps appears obvious that there are two elements involved, namely the overarching aspect of Artificial Intelligence (AI) along with a presumed intertwining somehow with the law (you already know about the law, due to serving as practicing attorneys or acting in other legal capacities). Since AI for you is ostensibly the least understood element of the two, you can go with a somewhat simple definition of AI for now, whereby AI is any machine or computer-based system that can be made to exhibit intelligent behavior.

I realize that seems a bit scant and could encompass a motley slew of possibilities.

I've previously provided an in-depth analysis of definitions about AI as covered in my columns, including this formalized statement from a regulation passed by the U.S. Congress: "An artificial system developed in computer software, physical hardware, or another context that solves tasks requiring human-like perception, cognition, planning, learning, communication, or physical action." As pointed out in my probing analysis, there is a lot of mushiness and ambiguity about AI and we will undoubtedly soon enough see court cases debating this rather loosey-goosey conundrum.

Another convenient approach to grasping what AI consists of would be to think about the various techniques and technologies that underlie today's AI capabilities. Keep in mind that there isn't any AI of today that is sentient. Not even close. We are a long and dusty trail away from being able to achieve the revered or feared sci-fi semblance of AI.

In any case, here are the typical computer techniques and technologies that fit in the overarching umbrella known as AI:

- Machine Learning (ML)
- Knowledge-Based Systems (KBS)
- Natural Language Processing (NLP)
- Computer Vision (CV)
- Robotics / Autonomy
- Common-Sense Reasoning (CSR)
- Other Advanced Technologies

The next facet about AI and the law is to realize that this a two-way street, as it were. You can apply AI to the law, which is one of the avenues to be pursued. The other way to go is to focus on the law as it applies to AI. Those two paths are crucial in their own independent way. In addition, they ultimately are interrelated. Envision these as the classic yin and yang, each chasing the tail of the other.

Okay, so we have this:
- AI as applied to the law
- The law as applied to AI

I'd bet that the notion of AI being applied to the law is what comes immediately to your mind when contemplating AI and the law. You've probably seen in the news and undoubtedly been approached by LegalTech vendors that claim they have infused AI into their wares. The aim of applying AI to the law is usually focused on adding AI or intelligent-like capabilities into otherwise conventional legal-oriented law office computer systems.

For example, conventional CLM (contract lifecycle management) software provides features to store contracts, modify contracts, keep track of contracts, and so on. AI-infused CLM tries to move things up a step and allow for "smart" capabilities such as having the AI identify what contracts are best for a given legal situation or that automatically assesses a contract for whatever loopholes or gotchas it might contain.

Taking all of that to a further extreme, there are efforts afoot to ultimately craft AI that can perform on par with human lawyers. This makes use of AI Legal Reasoning (AILR) and seeks to attain autonomous levels of machine-based lawyering.

Though I dislike the catchphrase of robo-lawyer, that is nonetheless a well-known moniker for those aspirations.

To provide some clarity about applying AI to the law, we can consider the host of legal efforts that are getting AI supplemental capabilities:

- Contracts Management
- Courts and Trials
- Documents and Records
- eDiscovery
- Intellectual Property (IP)
- Law Office Practice
- Lawyer & Client Interaction
- Legal Assistants
- Legal Case Management
- Legal Collaboration
- Legal Research
- Legal Workflow
- Legal Writing
- Professional Conduct
- Other

For my coverage on the full range of AI and law topics, see my book entitled "AI and Legal Reasoning Essentials" available on Amazon.

Other Side Of The Coin

We've briefly now covered the predominant one-way view of AI and the law, so let's consider the other one-way perspective consisting of a vaunted view about *the law as applied to AI*. This doesn't seem to be getting quite the same glamor and glitz as does AI applied to the law, though it is increasingly becoming a pressing topic. You can amply anticipate that it will get hotter and hotter as AI systems continue to be fostered upon us all.

The law as applied to AI is generally composed of two monumental questions:

- Do present-day laws properly and sufficiently encompass AI from a governance and regulatory perspective?
- Can or should AI have human rights?

Those are both veritable cans of worms. For example, some vehemently assert that AI will never rise to the full-on nature of humans and the human spirit, thus it is preposterous to suggest that AI will potentially need a semblance of human rights. Others disagree and have floated drafts depicting the customization of human rights toward that of AI and intelligent machines.

Probably the more down-to-earth facet of applying the law to AI consists of the concerns that existing laws are unfortunately weak or woefully outdated when it comes to guiding the legal limits and constraints needed to oversee AI systems. For example, AI systems have been placed into use that exhibits undue biases related to race, gender, etc. Some believe that those AI systems can get away with this scandalous activity because today's laws are silent or able to be skirted by sneaky ploys.

Perhaps our existing laws need to be amplified or augmented to make sure that AI assures:

- Human Dignity
- Human Freedom and Autonomy
- Prevention Of Harm
- Non-Discrimination, Gender Equality, Fairness, and Diversity
- Transparency and Explainability of AI Systems
- Data Protection and the Right To Privacy
- Accountability and Responsibility
- Democracy
- Rule of Law

Conclusion

On a final note about AI and the law, I mentioned earlier that the two paths are intertwined. This makes indubitable sense. For AI that is applied to the law, you would certainly hope that the AI is being governed or regulated as to being lawfully compliant. For law that is applied to AI, any AI should be legally bounded, and thus this naturally and of necessity includes AI as applied to the law.

I suppose you could say it is the grand circle of life, though admittedly maybe that's a bit of overstretched *The Lion King* kumbaya.

Note: *For supplemental materials depicting the aspects discussed in this chapter, refer to Appendix B, which contains various augmented diagrams, charts, and additional related facets of relevance.*

APPENDIX A

TEACHING WITH THIS MATERIAL AND BIBLIOGRAPHY

The essays in this book can readily be used as a reading supplemental to augment traditional textbook-oriented content, particularly used in a class on AI or a class about the law.

Courses where this material is most likely applicable encompass classes at a college or university level.

Here are some typical settings that might apply:

o   Computer Science. Classes studying AI, or possibly a CS social impacts class, etc.

o   Law. Law classes exploring technology and its adoption for legal uses.

o   Sociology. Sociology classes on the adoption and advancement of technology.

Specialized classes at the undergraduate and graduate level can also make use of this material.

For each chapter, consider whether you think the chapter provides material relevant to your course topic.

There are plenty of opportunities to get the students thinking about the topics and encourage them to decide whether they agree or disagree with the points offered and positions taken.

I would also encourage you to have the students do additional research beyond the chapter material presented (I provide next some suggested assignments that they can do).

RESEARCH ASSIGNMENTS ON THESE TOPICS

Your students can find research and background material on these topics, doing so in various tech journals, law journals, and other related publications.

Here are some suggestions for homework or projects that you could assign to students:

a) <u>Assignment for foundational AI research topics</u>: Research and prepare a paper and a presentation on a specific aspect of AI, such as Machine Learning, ANN, etc. The paper should cite at least 3 reputable sources. Compare and contrast to what has been stated in the chosen chapter.

b) <u>Assignment for Law topics</u>: Research and prepare a paper covering Law aspects via at least 3 reputable sources and analyze the characterizations. Compare and contrast to what has been stated in the chosen chapter.

c) <u>Assignment for a Business topic</u>: Research and prepare a paper and a presentation on businesses and advanced technology regarding AI and Law. What is trending, and why? Make sure to cite at least 3 reputable sources. Compare and contrast to the depictions herein.

d) <u>Assignment to do a Startup:</u> Have the students prepare a paper or business plan about how they might start up a business in this realm. They could also be asked to present their business plan and should also have a prepared presentation deck to coincide with it.

You can certainly adjust the aforementioned assignments to fit your particular needs and class structure.

You'll notice that I usually suggest that (at least) 3 reputable cited sources be utilized for the paper writing-based assignments.

I usually steer students toward "reputable" publications, since otherwise, they will cite some less reliable sources that have little or no credentials, other than that they happened to appear online was easy to retrieve. You can, of course, define "reputable" in whatever way you prefer, for example, some faculty think Wikipedia is not reputable while others believe it is reputable and allow students to cite it.

The reason that I usually ask for at least 3 citations is that if the student only relies upon one or two citations, they usually settle on whatever they happened to find the fastest. By requiring 3 (or more) citations, it usually seems to inspire them to explore more extensively and likely end-up finding five or more sources, and then whittling it down to 3 if so needed.

I have not specified the length of their papers and leave that to you to tell the students what you prefer.

For each of those assignments, you could end up with a short one to two-pager or you could do a dissertation length in-depth paper. Base the length on whatever best fits for your class, and likewise the credit amount of the assignment within the context of the other grading metrics you'll be using for the class.

I usually try to get students to present their work, in addition to doing the writing. This is a helpful practice for what they will do in the business world. Most of the time, they will be required to prepare an analysis and present it. If you don't have the class time or inclination to have the students present their papers, then you can presumably omit the aspect of them putting together presentations.

GUIDE TO USING THE CHAPTERS

For each of the chapters, I provide the next some various ways to use the chapter contents.

You can assign the below tasks as individual homework assignments, or the tasks can be used for team projects. You can easily layout a series of assignments, such as indicating that the students are to do item "a" below for say Chapter 1, then "b" for the next chapter of the book, and so on.

a) What is the main point of the chapter and describe in your own words the significance of the topic.

b) Identify at least two aspects in the chapter that you agree with and support your concurrence by providing at least one other outside researched item as support; make sure to explain your basis for agreeing with the aspects.

c) Identify at least two aspects in the chapter that you disagree with and support your disagreement by providing at least one other outside researched item as support; make sure to explain your basis for disagreeing with the aspects.

d) Find an aspect that was not covered extensively in the chapter, doing so by conducting outside research, and then offer an expanded indication about how that aspect ties into the chapter, along with the added significance it brings to the topic.

e) Interview a specialist in the industry about the topic of the chapter, collect from them their thoughts and opinions, and readdress the chapter by citing your source and how they compared and contrasted to the material,

f) Interview a relevant professor or researcher in a college or university setting about the topic of the chapter, collect from them their thoughts and opinions, and readdress the chapter by citing your source and how they compared and contrasted to the material,

g) Try to update a chapter by finding out the latest on the topic and ascertain whether the issue or topic has now been solved or whether it is still being addressed, explain what you come up with.

The above are all ways in which you can get the students of your class involved in considering the material of a given chapter. You could mix things up by having one of those above assignments per each week, covering the chapters over the course of the semester or quarter.

SUGGESTED REFERENCES TO EXPLORE

To help get your students started in finding relevant and important papers on the topic of AI and the law, I provide next a handy bibliography that can be utilized.

You could also assign the students to each (or in teams) read an assigned reference from the list, and then have them provide either a written summary and review or do so as part of a classroom presentation.

BIBLIOGRAPHIC REFERENCES

1. Aleven, Vincent (1997). "Teaching Case-Based Argumentation Through a Model and Examples," Ph.D. Dissertation, University of Pittsburgh.

2. Aleven, Vincent (2003). "Using Background Knowledge in Case-Based Legal Reasoning: A Computational Model and an Intelligent Learning Environment," Artificial Intelligence.

3. Amgoud, Leila (2012). "Five Weaknesses of ASPIC+," Volume 299, Communications in Computer and Information Science (CCIS).

4. Antonious, Grigoris, and George Baryannis, Sotiris Batsakis, Guido Governatori, Livio Robaldo, Givoanni Siragusa, Ilias Tachmazidis (2018). "Legal Reasoning and Big Data: Opportunities and Challenges," August 2018, MIREL Workshop on Mining and Reasoning Legal Texts.

5. Ashley, Kevin (1991). "Reasoning with Cases and Hypotheticals in HYPO," Volume 34, International Journal of Man-Machine Studies.

6. Ashley, Kevin, and Karl Branting, Howard Margolis, and Cass Sunstein (2001). "Legal Reasoning and Artificial Intelligence: How Computers 'Think' Like Lawyers," Symposium: Legal Reasoning and Artificial Intelligence, University of Chicago Law School Roundtable.

7. Baker, Jamie (2018). "A Legal Research Odyssey: Artificial Intelligence as Disrupter," Law Library Journal.

8. Batsakis, Sotiris, and George Baryannis, Guido Governatori, Illias Tachmazidis, Grigoris Antoniou (2018). "Legal Representation and Reasoning in Practice: A Critical Comparison," Volume 313, Legal Knowledge and Information Systems.

9. Bench-Capon, Trevor (2004). "AGATHA: Automation of the Construction of Theories in Case Law Domains," January 2004, Legal Knowledge and Information Systems Jurix 2004, Amsterdam.

10. Bench-Capon, Trevor (2012). "Representing Popov v Hayashi with Dimensions and Factors," March 2012, Artificial Intelligence and Law.

11. Bench-Capon, Trevor, and Givoanni Sartor (2003). "A Model of Legal Reasoning with Cases Incorporating Theories and Values," November 2013, Artificial Intelligence.

12. Breuker, Joost (1996). "A Functional Ontology of Law," October 1996, ResearchGate.

13. Bruninghaus, Stefanie, and Kevin Ashley (2003). "Combining Case-Based and Model-Based Reasoning for Predicting the Outcome of Legal Cases," June 2003, ICCBR'03: Proceedings of the 5th International Conference on Case-based reasoning: Research and Development.

14. Buchanan, Bruce, and Thomas Headrick (1970). "Some Speculation about Artificial Intelligence and Legal Reasoning," Volume 23, Stanford Law Review.

15. Chagal-Feferkorn, Karni (2019). "Am I An Algorithm or a Product: When Products Liability Should Apply to Algorithmic Decision-Makers," Stanford Law & Policy Review.

16. Douglas, William (1948). "The Dissent: A Safeguard of Democracy," Volume 32, Journal of the American Judicature Society.

17. Dung, P, and R. Kowalski, F. Toni (2006). "Dialectic Proof Procedures for Assumption-Based Admissible Argumentation," Artificial Intelligence.

18. Eliot, Lance (2020). AI And Legal Reasoning Essentials. LBE Press Publishing.

19. Eliot, Lance (2020). Artificial Intelligence and LegalTech Essentials. LBE Press Publishing.

20. Eliot, Lance (2020). Decisive Essays on AI and Law. LBE Press Publishing.

21. Eliot, Lance (2020). Incisive Research on AI and Law. LBE Press Publishing.

22. Eliot, Lance (2020). Ingenious Essays on AI and Law. LBE Press Publishing.

23. Eliot, Lance (2020). "FutureLaw 2020 Showcases How Tech is Transforming The Law, Including the Impacts of AI," April 16, 2020, Forbes.

24. Erdem, Esra, and Michael Gelfond, Nicola Leone (2016). "Applications of Answer Set Programming," AI Magazine.

25. Gardner, Anne (1987). Artificial Intelligence and Legal Reasoning. MIT Press.

26. Genesereth, Michael (2009). "Computational Law: The Cop in the Backseat," Stanford Center for Legal Informatics, Stanford University.

27. Ghosh, Mirna (2019). "Automation of Legal Reasoning and Decision Based on Ontologies," Normandie Universite.

28. Grabmair, Matthias (2017). "Predicting Trade Secret Case Outcomes using Argument Schemes and Learned Quantitative Value Effect Tradeoffs," IJCAI June 12, 2017, London, United Kingdom.

29. Hage, Jaap (1996). "A Theory of Legal Reasoning and a Logic to Match," Volume 4, Artificial Intelligence and Law.
30. Hage, Jaap (2000). "Dialectical Models in Artificial Intelligence and Law," Artificial Intelligence and Law.

31. Hage, Japp, and Ronald Leenes, Arno Lodder (1993). "Hard Cases: A Procedural Approach," Artificial Intelligence and Law.

32. Hobbes, Thomas (1651). The Matter, Form, and Power of a Common-Wealth Ecclesiasticall and Civil.

33. Holmes, Oliver (1897). "The Path of the Law," Volume 10, Harvard Law Review.

34. Katz, Daniel, and Michael Bommarito, Josh Blackman (2017). "A General Approach for Predicting the Behavior of the Supreme Court of the United States," April 12, 2017, PLOS ONE.

35. Kowalski, Robert, and Francesca Toni (1996). "Abstract Argumentation," AI-Law96.

36. Laswell, Harold (1955). "Current Studies of the Decision Process: Automation Creativity," Volume 8, Western Political Quarterly.

37. Libal, Tomer, and Alexander Steen (2019). "The NAI Suite: Drafting and Reasoning over Legal Texts," October 15, 2019, arXiv.

38. Lipton, Zachary (2017). "The Mythos of Model Interpretability," March 6, 2017, arXiv.

39. Martin, Andrew, and Kevin Quinn, Theodore Ruger, Pauline Kim (2004). "Competing Approaches to Predicting Supreme Court Decision Making," December 2014, Symposium on Forecasting U.S. Supreme Court Decisions.

40. McCarty, Thorne (1977). "Reflections on TAXMAN: An Experiment in Artificial Intelligence and Legal Reasoning," January 1977, Harvard Law Review.

41. Modgil, Sanjay, and Henry Prakken (2013). "The ASPIC+ Framework for Structured Argumentation: A Tutorial," December 16, 2013, Argument & Computation.

42. Mowbray, Andrew, and Philip Chung, Graham Greenleaf (2019). "Utilising AI in the Legal Assistance Sector," LegalAIIA Workshop, ICAIL, June 17, 2019, Montreal, Canada.

43. Parasuraman, Raja, and Thomas Sheridan, Christopher Wickens (2000). "A Model for Types and Levels of Human Interaction with Automation," May 2000, IEEE Transactions on Systems, Man, and Cybernetics.

44. Popple, James (1993). "SHYSTER: A Pragmatic Legal Expert System," Ph.D. Dissertation, Australian National University.

45. Prakken, Henry, and Giovanni Sartor (2015). "Law and Logic: A Review from an Argumentation Perspective," Volume 227, Artificial Intelligence.

46. Rissland, Edwina (1988). Artificial Intelligence and Legal Reasoning: A Discussion of the Field and Gardner's Book," Volume 9, AI Magazine.

47. Rissland, Edwina (1990). "Artificial Intelligence and Law: Stepping Stones to a Model of Legal Reasoning," Yale Law Journal.

48. Searle, John (1980). "Minds, Brains, and Programs," Volume 3, Behavioral and Brain Sciences.

49. Sunstein, Cass (2001). "Of Artificial Intelligence and Legal Reasoning," University of Chicago Law School, Public Law and Legal Theory Working Papers.

50. Sunstein, Cass, and Kevin Ashley, Karl Branting, Howard Margolis (2001). "Legal Reasoning and Artificial Intelligence: How Computers 'Think' Like Lawyers," Symposium: Legal Reasoning and Artificial Intelligence, University of Chicago Law School Roundtable.

51. Surden, Harry (2014). "Machine Learning and Law," Washington Law Review.

52. Surden, Harry (2019). "Artificial Intelligence and Law: An Overview," Summer 2019, Georgia State University Law Review.

53. Valente, Andre, and Joost Breuker (1996). "A Functional Ontology of Law," Artificial Intelligence and Law.

54. Waltl, Bernhard, and Roland Vogl (2018). "Explainable Artificial Intelligence: The New Frontier in Legal Informatics," February 2018, Jusletter IT 22, Stanford Center for Legal Informatics, Stanford University.

55. Wittgenstein, Ludwig (1953). Philosophical Investigations. Blackwell Publishing.

APPENDIX B
SUPPLEMENTAL
FIGURES AND CHARTS

For the convenience of viewing, supplemental figures and charts related to the topics discussed are shown on the next pages

Dr. Lance B. Eliot

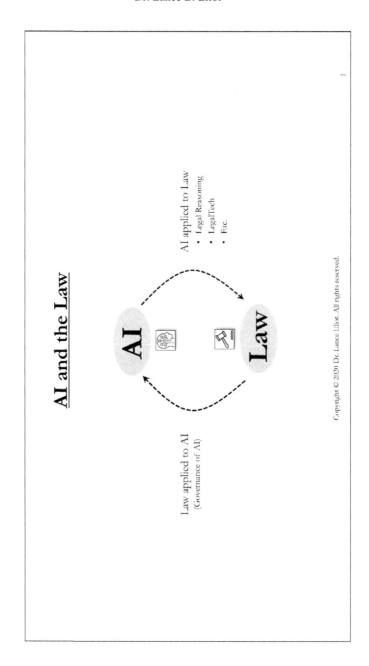

Figure 1

134

AI & Law: Levels of Autonomy For AI Legal Reasoning (AILR)

Level	Descriptor	Examples	Automation	Status
0	No Automation	Manual, paper-based (no automation)	None	De Facto - In Use
1	Simple Assistance Automation	Word Processing, XLS, online legal docs, etc.	Legal Assist	Widely In Use
2	Advanced Assistance Automation	Query-style NLP, ML for case prediction, etc.	Legal Assist	Some In Use
3	Semi-Autonomous Automation	KBS & ML/DL for legal reasoning & analysis, etc.	Legal Assist	Primarily Prototypes & Research Based
4	AILR Domain Autonomous	Versed only in a specific legal domain	Legal Advisor (law fluent)	None As Yet
5	AILR Fully Autonomous	Versatile within and across all legal domains	Legal Advisor (law fluent)	None As Yet
6	AILR Superhuman Autonomous	Exceeds human-based legal reasoning	Supra Legal Advisor	Indeterminate

V1.3

Source Author: Dr. Lance B. Eliot

Figure 1: AI & Law - Autonomous Levels by Rows

Figure 2

AI & Law: Levels of Autonomy For AI Legal Reasoning (AILR)

	Level 0	Level 1	Level 2	Level 3	Level 4	Level 5	Level 6
Descriptor	No Automation	Simple Assistance Automation	Advanced Assistance Automation	Semi-Autonomous Automation	AILR Domain Autonomous	AILR Fully Autonomous	AILR Superhuman Autonomous
Examples	Manual, paper-based (no automation)	Word Processing, XLS, online legal docs, etc.	Query-style NLP, ML for case prediction, etc.	KBS & ML/DL for legal reasoning & analysis, etc.	Versed only in a specific legal domain	Versatile within and across all legal domains	Exceeds human-based legal reasoning
Automation	None	Legal Assist	Legal Assist	Legal Assist	Legal Advisor (law fluent)	Legal Advisor (law fluent)	Supra Legal Advisor
Status	De Facto – In Use	Widely In Use	Some In Use	Primarily Prototypes & Research-based	None As Yet	None As Yet	Indeterminate

V1.3

Figure 2: AI & Law - Autonomous Levels by Columns

Source Author: Dr. Lance B. Eliot

Figure 3

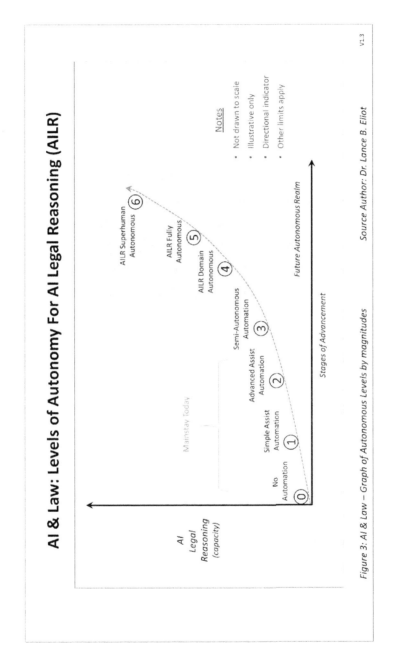

Figure 3: AI & Law – Graph of Autonomous Levels by magnitudes

Figure 4

Dr. Lance B. Eliot

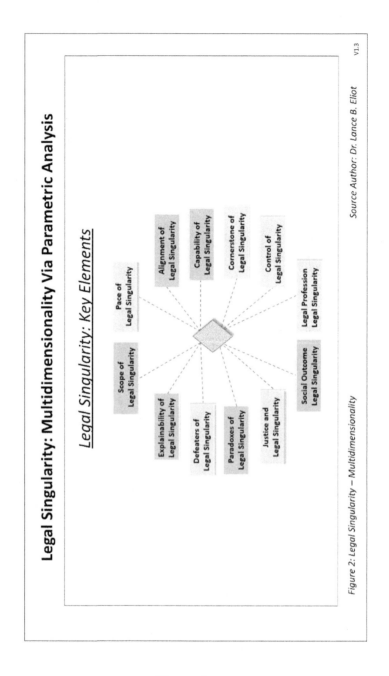

Figure 2: Legal Singularity – Multidimensionality

Figure 5

138

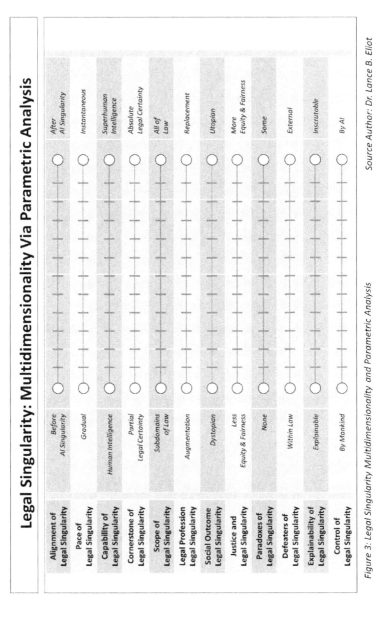

Figure 3:: Legal Singularity Multidimensionality and Parametric Analysis

Source Author: Dr. Lance B. Eliot

Figure 6

Legal Micro-Directives: Levels of Autonomy For AI Legal Reasoning (AILR)

	Level 0	Level 1	Level 2	Level 3	Level 4	Level 5	Level 6
Descriptor	No Automation	Simple Assistance Automation	Advanced Assistance Automation	Semi-Autonomous Automation	AILR Domain Autonomous	AILR Fully Autonomous	AILR Superhuman Autonomous
Examples	Manual, paper-based (no automation)	Word Processing, XLS, online legal docs, etc.	Query-style NLP, ML for case prediction, etc.	KBS & ML/DL for legal reasoning & analysis, etc.	Versed only in a specific legal domain	Versatile within and across all legal domains	Exceeds human-based legal reasoning
Automation	None	Legal Assist	Legal Assist	Legal Assist	Legal Advisor (law fluent)	Legal Advisor (law fluent)	Supra Legal Advisor
Status	De Facto – In Use	Widely In Use	Some In Use	Primarily Prototypes & Research-based	None As Yet	None As Yet	Indeterminate
AI-Enabled Legal Micro-Directives	n/a	Impractical	Incubatory	Infancy	Narrow	Wide	Consummate

V1.3

Source Author: Dr. Lance B. Eliot

Figure 1: Legal Micro-Directives - Autonomous Levels of AILR by Columns

Figure 7

140

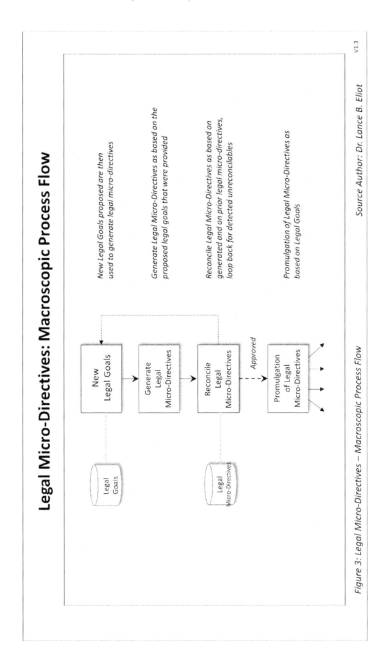

Figure 3: Legal Micro-Directives – Macroscopic Process Flow

Figure 8

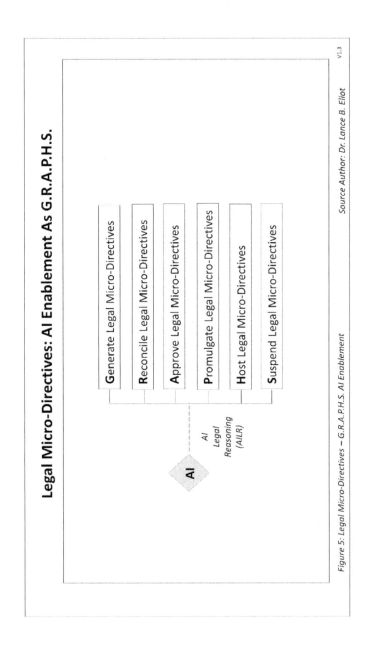

Figure 9

Legal Argumentation: Levels of Autonomy For AI Legal Reasoning (AILR)

	Level 0	Level 1	Level 2	Level 3	Level 4	Level 5	Level 6
Descriptor	No Automation	Simple Assistance Automation	Advanced Assistance Automation	Semi-Autonomous Automation	AILR Domain Autonomous	AILR Fully Autonomous	AILR Superhuman Autonomous
Examples	Manual, paper-based (no automation)	Word Processing, XLS, online legal docs, etc.	Query-style NLP, ML for case prediction, etc.	KBS & ML/DL for legal reasoning & analysis, etc.	Versed only in a specific legal domain	Versatile within and across all legal domains	Exceeds human-based legal reasoning
Automation	None	Legal Assist	Legal Assist	Legal Assist	Legal Advisor (law fluent)	Legal Advisor (law fluent)	Supra Legal Advisor
Status	De Facto – In Use	Widely In Use	Some In Use	Primarily Prototypes & Research-based	None As Yet	None As Yet	Indeterminate
AI-Enabled Legal Argumentation	n/a	Mechanistic (Low)	Mechanistic (High)	Expressive	Domain Fluency	Full Fluency	Meta-Fluency

V1.3

Figure 7: AI Legal Argumentation (AILA) - Autonomous Levels of AILR by Columns

Source Author: Dr. Lance B. Eliot

Figure 10

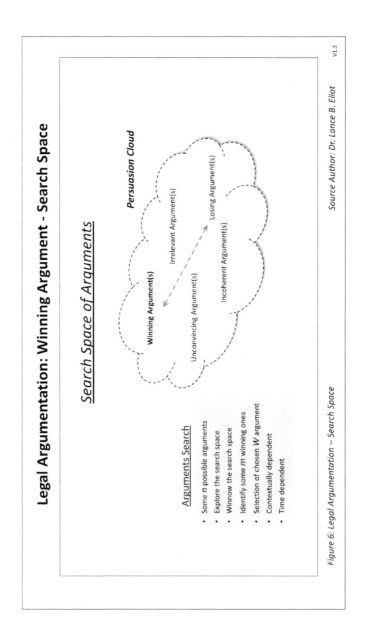

Figure 11

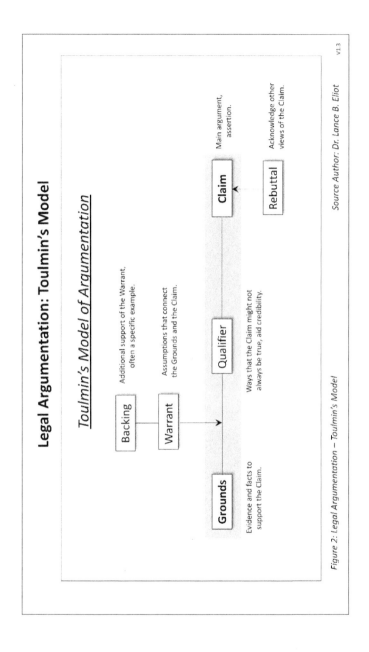

Figure 2: Legal Argumentation – Toulmin's Model

Figure 12

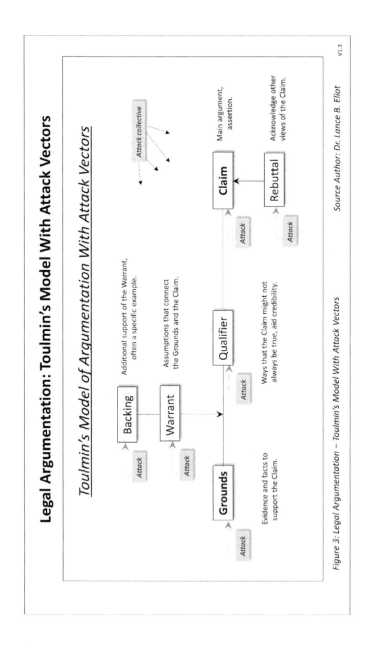

Figure 13

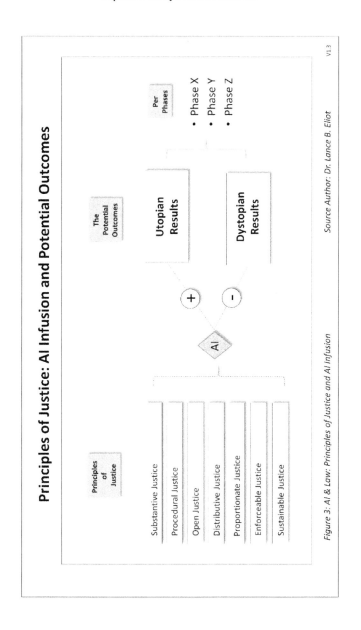

Figure 14

Principles of Justice and Autonomous Levels of AI Legal Reasoning (AILR)

Descriptor	Level 0 No Automation	Level 1 Simple Assistance Automation	Level 2 Advanced Assistance Automation	Level 3 Semi-Autonomous Automation	Level 4 AILR Domain Autonomous	Level 5 AILR Fully Autonomous	Level 6 AILR Superhuman Autonomous
Substantive Justice	Traditional	Traditional	Traditional	Emerging	Phase X Impacts	Phase Y Impacts	Phase Z Impacts
Procedural Justice	Traditional	Traditional	Traditional	Emerging	Phase X Impacts	Phase Y Impacts	Phase Z Impacts
Open Justice	Traditional	Traditional	Traditional	Emerging	Phase X Impacts	Phase Y Impacts	Phase Z Impacts
Distributive Justice	Traditional	Traditional	Traditional	Emerging	Phase X Impacts	Phase Y Impacts	Phase Z Impacts
Proportionate Justice	Traditional	Traditional	Traditional	Emerging	Phase X Impacts	Phase Y Impacts	Phase Z Impacts
Enforceable Justice	Traditional	Traditional	Traditional	Emerging	Phase X Impacts	Phase Y Impacts	Phase Z Impacts
Sustainable Justice	Traditional	Traditional	Traditional	Emerging	Phase X Impacts	Phase Y Impacts	Phase Z Impacts

V1.3

Source Author: Dr. Lance B. Eliot

Figure 1: AI & Law – Principles of Justice and LoA AILR by Columns

Figure 15

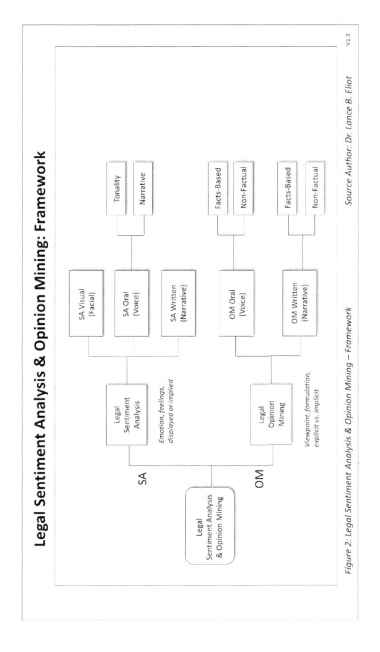

Figure 16

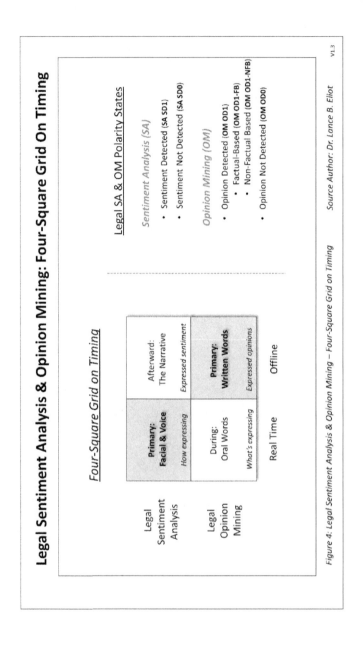

Figure 17

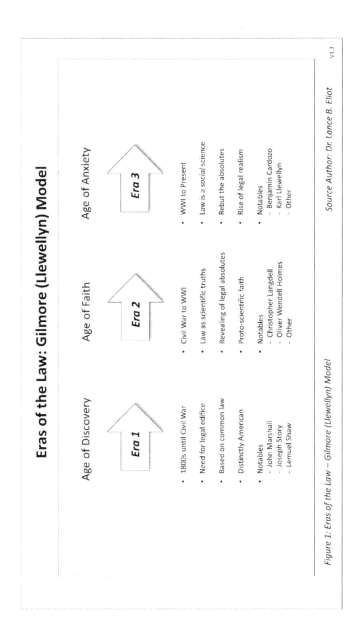

Figure 1: Eras of the Law – Gilmore (Llewellyn) Model

Figure 18

Dr. Lance B. Eliot

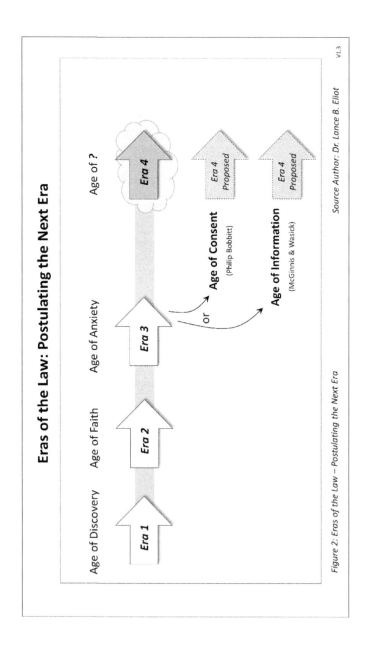

Figure 19

152

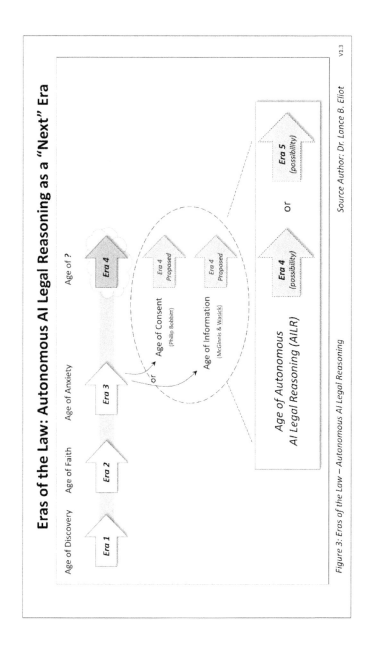

Figure 20

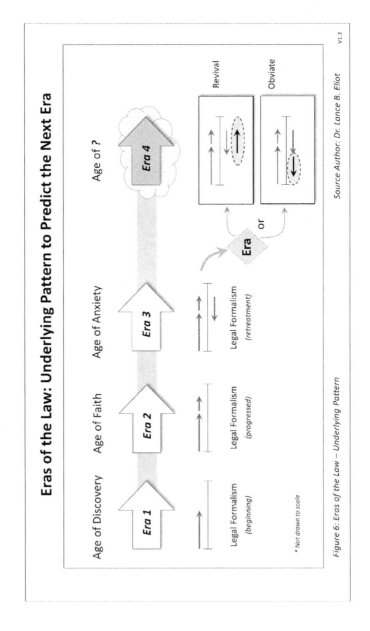

Figure 21

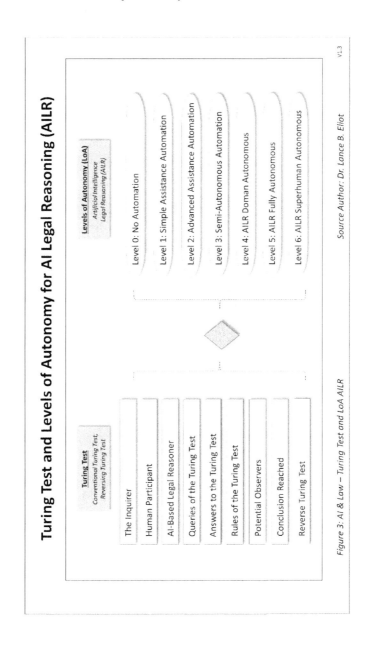

Figure 3: AI & Law – Turing Test and LoA AILR

Source Author: Dr. Lance B. Eliot

Figure 22

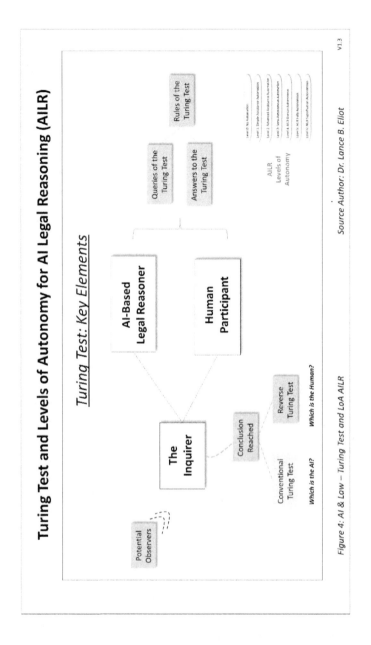

Figure 23

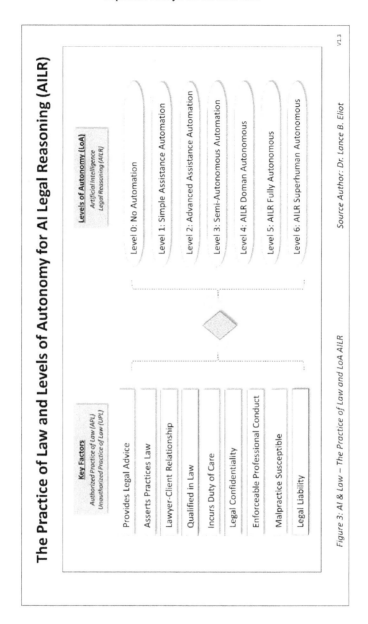

Figure 24

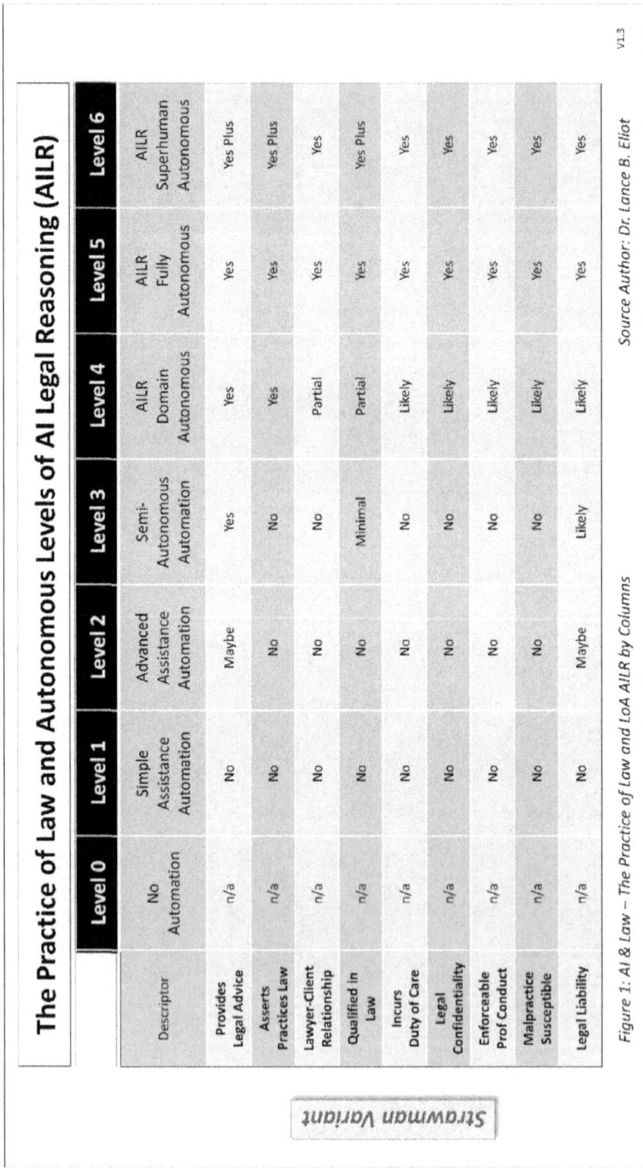

The Practice of Law and Autonomous Levels of AI Legal Reasoning (AILR)

Descriptor	Level 0 No Automation	Level 1 Simple Assistance Automation	Level 2 Advanced Assistance Automation	Level 3 Semi-Autonomous Automation	Level 4 AILR Domain Autonomous	Level 5 AILR Fully Autonomous	Level 6 AILR Superhuman Autonomous
Provides Legal Advice	n/a	No	Maybe	Yes	Yes	Yes	Yes Plus
Asserts Practices Law	n/a	No	No	No	Yes	Yes	Yes Plus
Lawyer-Client Relationship	n/a	No	No	No	Partial	Yes	Yes
Qualified in Law	n/a	No	No	Minimal	Partial	Yes	Yes Plus
Incurs Duty of Care	n/a	No	No	No	Likely	Yes	Yes
Legal Confidentiality	n/a	No	No	No	Likely	Yes	Yes
Enforceable Prof Conduct	n/a	No	No	No	Likely	Yes	Yes
Malpractice Susceptible	n/a	No	No	No	Likely	Yes	Yes
Legal Liability	n/a	No	Maybe	Likely	Likely	Yes	Yes

V1.3

Strawman Variant

Figure 1: AI & Law – The Practice of Law and LoA AILR by Columns

Source Author: Dr. Lance B. Eliot

Figure 25

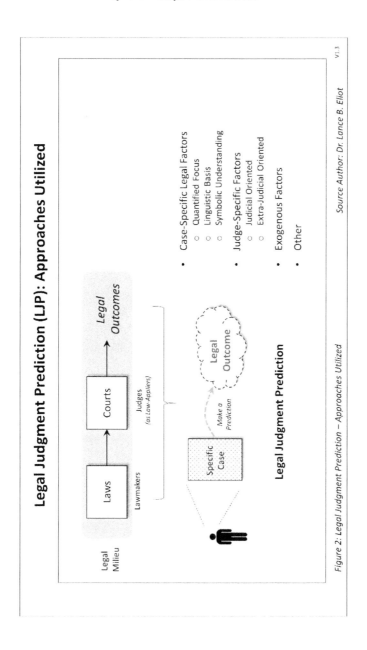

Figure 26

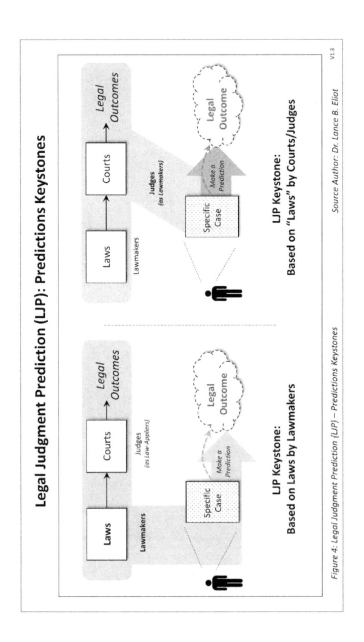

Figure 27

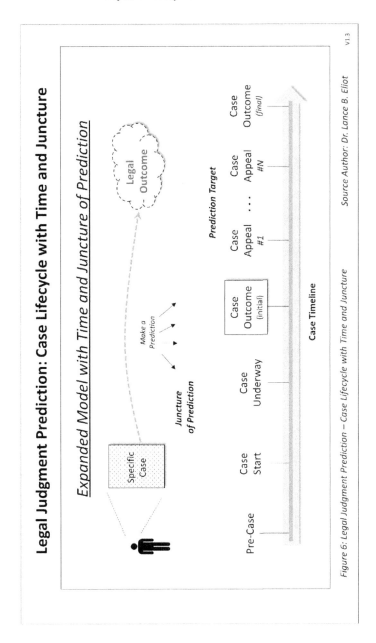

Figure 28

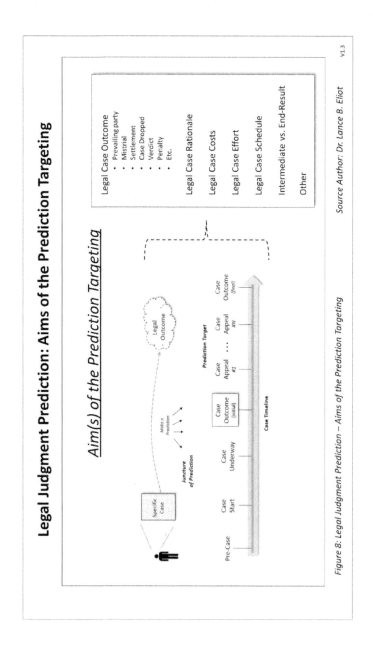

Figure 29

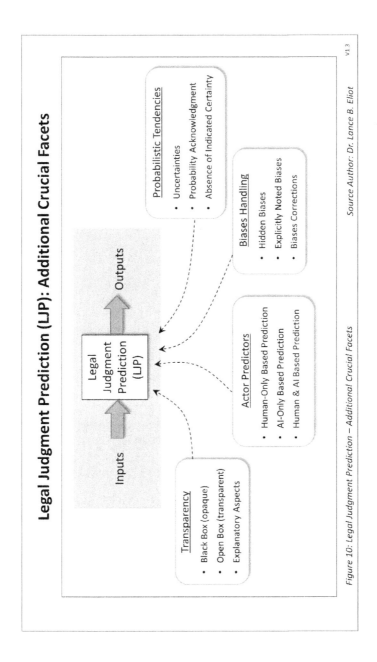

Figure 10: Legal Judgment Prediction – Additional Crucial Facets

Figure 30

Dr. Lance B. Eliot

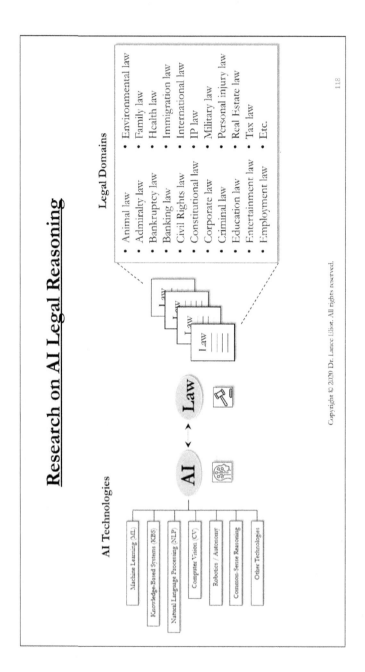

Figure 31

164

ABOUT THE AUTHOR

Dr. Lance B. Eliot, Ph.D., MBA is a globally recognized AI expert and thought leader, an invited Stanford Fellow at Stanford University, an experienced top executive and corporate leader, a successful entrepreneur, and a noted scholar on AI, including that his Forbes and AI Trends columns have amassed over 4 million views, his books on AI are ranked in the Top 10 of all-time AI books, his journal articles are widely cited, and he has developed and implemented numerous AI systems.

He currently serves as the Chief AI Scientist at Techbruim, Inc. and has over twenty years of industry experience including serving as a corporate officer in billion-dollar sized firms and was a partner in a major consulting firm. He is also a successful entrepreneur having founded, ran, and sold several high-tech related businesses.

Dr. Eliot previously hosted the popular radio show *Technotrends* that was also available on American Airlines flights via their in-flight audio program, he has made appearances on CNN, has been a frequent speaker at industry conferences, and his podcasts have been downloaded over 150,000 times.

A former professor at the University of Southern California (USC), he founded and led an innovative research lab on Artificial Intelligence. He also previously served on the faculty of the University of California Los Angeles (UCLA) and was a visiting professor at other major universities. He was elected to the International Board of the Society for Information Management (SIM), a prestigious association of over 3,000 high-tech executives worldwide.

He has performed extensive community service, including serving as Senior Science Adviser to the Congressional Vice-Chair of the Congressional Committee on Science & Technology. He has served on the Board of the OC Science & Engineering Fair (OCSEF), where he is also has been a Grand Sweepstakes judge, and likewise served as a judge for the Intel International SEF (ISEF). He served as the Vice-Chair of the Association for Computing Machinery (ACM) Chapter, a prestigious association of computer scientists. Dr. Eliot has been a shark tank judge for the USC Mark Stevens Center for Innovation on start-up pitch competitions and served as a mentor for several incubators and accelerators in Silicon Valley and in Silicon Beach.

Dr. Eliot holds a Ph.D. from USC, MBA, and Bachelor's in Computer Science, and earned the CDP, CCP, CSP, CDE, and CISA certifications

ADDENDUM

Thanks for reading this book and I hope you will continue your interest in the field of AI & Law

---

For my free podcasts about AI & Law:

https://ai-law.libsyn.com/website

Those podcasts are also available on Spotify, iTunes, etc.

For the latest on AI & Law see my website:

www.ai-law.legal

To follow me on Twitter:

https://twitter.com/LanceEliot

For my in-depth book on AI & Law:

AI And Legal Reasoning Essentials

www.amazon.com/gp/product/1734601655/

Printed in Great Britain
by Amazon

83563798R00102